Practical Knowledge
of the Soul

Practical Knowledge of the Soul

With a New Introduction
An Argo Book

EUGEN ROSENSTOCK-HUESSY

Translated by
Mark Huessy
and
Freya von Moltke

WIPF & STOCK · Eugene, Oregon

PRACTICAL KNOWLEDGE OF THE SOUL

Copyright © 2015 The Eugen Rosenstock-Huessy Fund. All rights reserved. Except for brief quotations in critical publications or reviews, no part of this book may be reproduced in any manner without prior written permission from the publisher. Write: Permissions, Wipf and Stock Publishers, 199 W. 8th Ave., Suite 3, Eugene, OR 97401.

Wipf & Stock
An Imprint of Wipf and Stock Publishers
199 W. 8th Ave., Suite 3
Eugene, OR 97401

www.wipfandstock.com

ISBN 13: 978-1-4982-8210-9

Manufactured in the U.S.A.

Readers wishing to learn more about the life and work of Eugen Rosenstock-Huessy should visit www.erhfund.org and www.erhsociety.org.

Contents

Foreword | *vii*

Introduction | *ix*

1. Practical Study of the Soul | 1
2. The Science of Psychology | 5
3. The Psyche | 9
4. The Occult Sciences | 12
5. The Grammar of the Soul | 18
6. The Fate of the Soul | 34
7. The Powers of the Soul | 39
8. Community | 44
9. The Speech of the Community | 48
10. Our People | 62
11. Spirit, Soul, and Body | 67
12. The Grammatical Method | 73

Foreword

THIS WORK WAS FIRST published in English in 1988 by Argo Books, under the auspices of the Eugen Rosenstock-Huessy Fund. The occasion was the one-hundredth anniversary of the author's birth. The work originated as a manuscript composed by Rosenstock-Huessy in 1916 for his friend and student, Franz Rosenzweig. Rosenzweig subsequently described it as providing "the main influence" for his epochal book, *Stern der Erlösung* (1920) (Star of Redemption).

A printed version of the text appeared in Germany in 1924 as *Angewandte Seelenkunde: Eine Programmatische Übersetzung*, published by Röther-Verlag in Darmstadt, and Rosenstock-Huessy later incorporated the work into his two-volume *Die Sprache des Menschengeschlects* (Heidelberg: Verlag Lambert Schneider, 1963) (The Speech of Humankind).

This new English edition issued by Wipf and Stock follows almost exactly the text of the 1988 version, as translated by Mark Huessy and Freya von Moltke. The editor of that first edition, Clinton C. Gardner, described it, however, as an "interim" publication, anticipating that eventually a more formal, polished book would be brought out. In that respect, this publication completely supersedes the 1988 version. As a matter of information, Gardner noted that in making their translation, although they started completely afresh, Huessy and von Moltke were able to "take advantage" of an earlier translation, never published, by Rolf von Eckartsberg.

Foreword

Gardner also credited Frances Huessy for the initial typing of the work.

Entirely new here is the Introduction. Written by Hans van der Heiden, Otto Kroesen, and Henk van Olst, it is a translation into English of the Introduction they prepared for the publication in 2014 of the translation into Dutch of *Angewandte Seleenkunde*. The English version is slightly modified from the original. In North America we have a Rosenstock-Huessy Society; in Germany, there is the Rosenstock-Huessy *Gesellschaft*; in the Netherlands, the Rosenstock-Huessy circle is called *Respondeo*, which is responsible for the new Dutch edition. It is gratifying for those in North America interested in Rosenstock-Huessy to be collaborating with *Respondeo* in this way.

Editorial Note

Editorial insertions in the text are enclosed in square brackets. Nearly all of the footnotes were supplied by the editor. The few footnotes written by Rosenstock-Huessy are preceded by "*ERH*".

N. F.

Introduction

LANGUAGE AS THE STARTING POINT OF THOUGHT

IN 1925 FRANZ ROSENZWEIG wrote an essay with the title "*Das neue Denken.*" (The New Thinking). In it he gave a sketch of the points of departure and background of his great three-part book *Der Stern der Erlösung.* (The Star of Redemption). In addition, he put this work within a broader horizon. Since that time, the term "*Sprach-denken,*" speech-thinking, has gained currency. This term indicates the new approach of a philosophy that starts from language instead of thought. Consider that our direct experience has already found names and words for things before our thought in reflection looks back on them. Most convincingly this is the case in our deepest experience, to love and to be loved. Before thought, love gives new names to things, people, and experiences. In that sense, experiences become revelations providing orientation. Our thoughts cannot deduce such experiences from a priori principles. Instead, it cannot do otherwise but follow language in its movement, and as such, thought becomes "*Sprach-denken,*" speech-thinking.

In this new way of assessing thinking and experience, Rosenzweig did not stand on his own. He participated in the discussions of a small group of friends, such as Eugen Rosenstock-Huessy, who

INTRODUCTION

were mostly emancipated and assimilated Jews, or converted Jews. In their many conversations and discussions as well as in their publications, they considered the entire religious and secular heritage of Europe and reflected on its meaning for their time. They were the first completely integrated Jewish generation in Germany after 1870, that is, after political unification, and they benefited from the strong economic and technological boost of this new state. They were in fact the first Jewish generation to participate fully in European culture.

Yet, at the peak of European imperial expansion they already had an inkling of the coming crisis and decay of this Europe. European imperialism for the first time brought about a global society, albeit in the form of colonies subjected to Western hegemony. The German Empire all of a sudden became a powerful economic and political player on the stage of this world theater. At the same time, catastrophe was imminent: the rise of socialism due to class divisions, the highly competitive rivalries in the search for markets, international power politics and coalitions of different power blocs. Many people already sensed that these tensions could not continue without dire consequences. Despite this anticipation, the world war that broke out in 1914 was a shattering experience. In one of his letters Rosenzweig wrote: "Around us the theater of this world has broken down." National states that took themselves as absolutes, for four years struggled against each other over life and death, as if they had not been already for a long time part of one Europe. Rosenstock-Huessy later said that already in the trenches of Verdun he had a vision of the ground plan of his book *Die Europäischen Revolutionen* (1931). In this book, as in the English-language sequel, *Out of Revolution* (1938), he presented European history as an ongoing dialogue between different national traditions, even if the countries did not like each other and it was unwitting. As part of this history they cannot take themselves anymore as absolutes, and they have something to say to each other of lasting value. That is the better option. That is what language does: People following the course of their own monologue are turned around to face each other and opened up to the discourse of the

INTRODUCTION

Other. Where people and traditions lack a common denominator, and violence lurks around the corner, language offers an escape. When we cannot deal with each other in any way anymore, we have to talk to escape violence. Whoever makes that discovery, discovers the peace-creating dimension of language, and it is this discovery that evokes the question: What is actually happening when people talk to each other? To talk, to speak, what actually does that mean?

Of course this also raises the question of speech in the conversations of this group of friends, of which Rosenstock-Huessy was a part. If people really speak to each other, in one way or another such a dialogue produces change. Speech is not in the first place simply the disclosure of information that is to be processed in our brains. Instead it is the word seeking an entry, via the ear, to our hearts. In the correspondence of Rosenstock-Huessy and Rosenzweig during the First World War, at one point Rosenzweig posed the question: Where are our languages coming from? To this question Rosenstock-Huessy provides an answer, quite extensively.

That answer is the kernel of this text. The manuscript was in 1916 sent as a letter from the Western front of the German army by Rosenstock-Huessy to his friend and partner in dialogue Franz Rosenzweig, stationed at the Eastern front in the Balkans. It is the oldest document of what later, thanks to Martin Buber who also belonged to this circle of friends, became known as the philosophy of dialogue. It had a decisive impact on the coming to birth of *Der Stern der Erlösung*. Rosenstock-Huessy reworked it and added to it, and in 1924 for the first time it was published, under the title *Angewandte Seelenkunde*. The standard title for the English version is *Practical Knowledge of the Soul*. The new Dutch translation has the title *The Language of the Soul* (*De taal van de ziel*, 2014).

When Rosenzweig started writing the *Stern* he already for one-and-a-half years was in possession of this text. In it for the first time Rosenstock-Huessy gave a sketch of his "grammatical method." In 1963 the great work of Eugen Rosenstock-Huessy *Die Sprache des Menschengeschlechts* (*The Speech of Mankind*) was published. At the end of the first volume of this work, *Angewandte*

Seelenkunde was once more printed, with some small additions, and it is that final German version that is the basis of this English edition. As noted, it is the first source document of the philosophy of dialogue, as Buber called it; of speech-thinking according to Rosenzweig; of the grammatical method according to Rosenstock-Huessy. We prefer the term "speech-sociology" rather than speech-thinking, because that is what Rosenstock-Huessy is after with his grammatical method. Speech groups and re-groups people. Speech when uttering the right thing keeps society healthy and creates right relations.

THE *SEELENKUNDE* AND THE *STERN*

The statement that this text was the basis and the impetus towards the writing of the *Stern* is not an exaggeration. Rosenzweig absorbed the work and when challenged by Rosenstock-Huessy to articulate his own point of view, acknowledged its influence. Of course, many ideas in the *Stern* can be traced back to conversations among this circle of friends, to such an extent that often it is not clear anymore whose contribution it first was. Nevertheless, *Angewandte Seelenkunde* was of decisive importance, particularly the part about revelation, or love, and the part about redemption, or prayer, or more precisely, the orientation of prayer.

In the first part of the *Stern*, Rosenzweig breaks with his own Hegelian past. He does not derive our knowledge from reason, but from not-knowing. We do not know God, we do not know man, and we do not know the world, but from this starting point of not-knowing a process begins by which we *learn* to know these different elements—actually from our living and for that reason also from our historical experience. Instead of the Hegelian dialectic self-movement of conceptual understanding, we might say, we now with Rosenzweig have the self-movement of non-understanding. Precisely because we do not understand, we follow our experience the better. This philosophical inquiry leads to the knowledge of three irreducible elements which—in whatever way we are moving—appear to be the structuring elements of

Introduction

our experience. First, some power disposes of us for better or for worse: God. Second, we experience a stubborn self-affirmation in our own person: man. Finally, there is the perpetual emergence of ever new surprises and events: the world. In a somewhat different form we also meet these three fundamental elements in *Practical Knowledge of the Soul*.

These three elements also describe the heritage of antiquity, the pre-Christian and pre-Jewish conception of God, man, and world. We see in antiquity the experience of the tragic but nevertheless stubborn self-affirming man. He experiences himself as subject to the power game of the gods and feels exposed to the arbitrariness of fate, but he tolerates this situation with inflexible perseverance or by patient conformity. The gods keep themselves aloof from human beings, and human beings cannot give themselves to each other. As a consequence the world can never become the cosmos it should be.

The influence of Rosenstock-Huessy can be particularly felt in the emphasis on the imperatival character of language: the commandment to love! That imperative appears when—as described in the second part of the *Stern*—a divine appeal and outreach lift me out of my stubborn self-sufficiency and turn me towards my neighboring fellow-man, to impart finally to the things in the world a new order. That is the event of revelation. The commandment to love is furthermore joined by prayer—as described in the third part of the *Stern*. Like the commandment to love, prayer is not about a particularly pious act, but rather about the direction of the new love and the coming into being of a new community giving support to it. In *Practical Knowledge of the Soul* Rosenstock-Huessy points to the relief and unburdening of the "I" in its response to a new imperative when others help and lend support. Awakened by the same imperative, people can support each other in responding to the new challenge. Precisely if I am not left alone in my personal responsibility, if others come to help in changing the world, something significant can be achieved. All great institutions have come into being in this way—the rule of law, parliamentary government, freedom of conscience, the nation-state,

INTRODUCTION

etc.—as Rosenstock-Huessy later delineated in his *Out of Revolution* (1938).

In *Practical Knowledge of the Soul* Rosenstock-Huessy calls upon the disoriented German people after the First World War to do something similar. Rosenzweig takes up this approach in his own way and points to the Jewish liturgy as the *final realization* of the redemption (that broadly is how prayer for the coming of the kingdom should be understood!). That stands in opposition to the Christian liturgy as the basis of another unique community which pulls us toward the redemption that is longed for but in a series of *temporary phases*.

As already stressed, *Practical Knowledge of the Soul* is not the exclusive source of the *Stern*. The circle of friends mentioned above evoked and shared many insights with each other. This circle can itself be viewed as such a new community, helping and supporting each other in response to a new imperative. But this help and support in a common task was—as is often the case in history— somewhat less harmonious than we might in the first instance be inclined to think. Each member of this circle eventually moved from this new imperative to a different front. As the etymology of the word "answer" itself indicates (it is derived from "anti-word"), to respond often means to oppose. Such was the case between Rosenstock-Huessy and Rosenzweig, but also between both of them and Martin Buber, and also, for another example, between Rudolf and Hans Ehrenberg. Furthermore Victor von Weizäcker, Ferdinand Ebner, and Florens Christian Rang should be mentioned as members of, or at least as more distant participants in, the group who followed different paths. Even Karl Barth temporarily belonged to the group. Hans Ehrenberg in particular put a lot of effort into drawing him in, had many conversations with him, and even functioned as the publisher of his famous *Tambacher Rede* (1920), presented at a congress of Christian socialists.

Rosenzweig, Buber, and Rosenstock-Huessy each cite Ludwig Feuerbach as the first discoverer of their way of thinking. Marx interpreted Feuerbach in a very one-sided way by framing him in his famous *Theses on Feuerbach* merely as an anti-metaphysical

INTRODUCTION

thinker. But Feuerbach had already interpreted the relation between human beings, that is, human dialogue, as a manifestation of God. God, when he disappeared as the guarantor of the cosmic order, immediately reappeared in social relationships. Rosenzweig also named his teacher in Berlin, the philosopher Herman Cohen, as one who anticipated speech-thinking as a philosophical method.

It is remarkable also that Franz Rosenzweig, Eugen Rosenstock-Huessy, and Ferdinand Ebner all invoke the thought of Johann Georg Hamann (1730-1788), who can be considered an elder predecessor of this new conception of language. Quite exceptionally in his time, Hamann put forward the priority of language above thought. In opposition to Kant and rationalistic philosophers like Moses Mendelssohn, he emphasized the creative power of language. We can only think, he said, on the basis of linguistic expressions that first have been articulated. The words and names we use, the body of language, is the creation of God. By language we live in God and God in us. Thus Hamann.

INDIRECT IMPACT ON THE WORK OF LEVINAS

Emmanuel Levinas (d. 1995) made a thorough study of the *Stern*, but the name, let alone the work, of Rosenstock-Huessy was wholly unknown to him. Nevertheless, we want to mention him in this introduction because his work is an example of how history can repeat itself. Rosenzweig turned against the totalitarian thought of nineteenth-century idealism, in particular Hegel. Following Rosenstock-Huessy, Rosenzweig emphasized the importance of language and love as sources of orientation, not as subject to the internal processes of reason, but from the outside. Similarly, Levinas turned against the totalitarian thought of Martin Heidegger (d. 1976). "Neutralizing" instead of "totalitarian" in this case might be the better term. His reproach to Heidegger was that he neutralized the appeal of the Other by keeping that appeal at a reflective distance and that his analysis of existence in this way remained ego-logy. He remained self-sufficient and indifferent and does not allow himself to be touched.

Levinas, on the contrary, emphasized the meaning of language. The kernel of language is responsibility; speaking is responding, and it is impossible to do otherwise. Just as Rosenstock-Huessy and Rosenzweig discovered the significance of speech under the pressure of the First World War, Levinas did so under the pressure of the Second World War. It was only after World War II that Levinas made an in-depth study of the work of Rosenzweig, and in his main work, published in 1961, *Totality and Infinity*, he stated that the influence of Rosenzweig was so often present in the book that it would be impossible to footnote. Without any doubt that is the case.

Levinas's opposition to totalitarian thinking and the emergence of the term "totality" itself, his criticism of impersonal reason, and his employment of the term "responsibility" to indicate the seriousness of love, also characterized Rosenzweig's writing about love. The presentation is in the style of Levinas, but the parallels with the work of Rosenzweig lie right beneath the surface. For Levinas, the social relationship is the concretization of the idea of Infinity. The totality cannot contain the idea of Infinity. In the same fashion, Rosenzweig indicated in the *Stern* that the elements of God, man, and world cannot be deduced from the principles of reason. On top of that, Levinas makes an appeal to Descartes, who also needs the idea of Infinity as a moral or metaphysical foundation for his rational research. Rosenzweig points to the endless tumbling of thought that, left to itself, does not know where to begin or end and that can never establish any definite meaning for anything. Levinas pointed to the experience which he called "there is," the experience of meaninglessness and senselessness. In distinction, the epiphany of the Other is an appeal to responsibility that makes sense and that creates meaning. In so arguing, Levinas finally provided an ethical foundation to postmodern thought, exposed as it is to endless and arbitrary constructions and deconstructions.

Introduction

Many notions that in the *Stern* are indicated only sketchily are concretized and elaborated in the work of Levinas with a more accurate phenomenological and conceptual apparatus. To one of these notions we would like to pay somewhat more attention. It is the notion of the "stubborn I," about which Rosenstock-Huessy speaks in *Practical Knowledge of the Soul* and that Rosenzweig adopts in the *Stern*. Rosenstock-Huessy uses this notion for the tragic human being who is appealed to by God and called to life, but refuses to answer, or postpones an answer. Yet it is by this appeal that he first discovers himself. Precisely the appeal from the Other calls the independent "I" awake! Even before he had studied the work of Rosenzweig, Levinas found in the "I" an independence that cannot be absorbed in reason or thinking or in the understanding of being (as Heidegger maintained), and which he called "hypostasis." Hypostasis makes itself felt in the experience of nausea or sleeplessness or fatigue, where one finds oneself riveted without a way out, as Levinas described it in *De l'existance à l'existant* (1947). You can be an obstacle to yourself, especially when you are nauseous. In his later work—*Autrement qu' être* (1974)—Levinas took up that thought once more: The way out of being riveted is to respond to the appeal that comes from the face of another. "To transcend oneself, to go out of one's comfort zone to such an extent as to leave one's self, that is, to put oneself in the place of the Other. In the bearing of myself not to bear myself, but, by the power of my being singled out as a unique person, expiate evil for the other." This responsibility is the inner core of my humanity and to speak is that same inner core. In another place, Levinas proposes his conception and translation of the commandment to love thy neighbor as thyself. He emphasizes that it is also possible to translate "love thy neighbor" to mean "love your neighbor, for that is what you are," which means that you consist of that love to the neighbor.

Speaking and responding are the inner core of my being before it crystallizes to a fixed identity and with that reverts to paganism. According to Rosenstock-Huessy, it is the apostle John who in the opening words of his gospel for the first time uncovers this divine nature of speech. He could not have done so if the

INTRODUCTION

tragic and "stubborn I" of antiquity had not been reversed, in the name of Christ, to love that gives the priority to the Other. In the crucifixion of Christ historically the transition takes place from the "stubborn I" to the responding "you" or "thou" who is addressed, a "you" that in its inner core consists of responsibility and substitution for-the-Other, in Levinas's terms. Levinas makes this discovery through an analysis of human existence. Precisely the atrocities of World War II and the responsibilities accepted by all sorts of ordinary people reveal this responsibility as an undeniable fact. Is that not striking and miraculous and at the same time proof of the inner unity of Judaism and Christianity?

This inner unity of Judaism and Christianity, this conversion towards each other and recognition of each other, only becomes an option by the meaning these traditions are given in the work and the dialogue of Rosenstock-Huessy and Rosenzweig. The work of Levinas can be understood as a fruit of this process. The reversal from the "stubborn I" towards the responding "you" is discovered by Rosenstock-Huessy as the essential transition from antiquity to the Christian era. It becomes part of the *Stern* of Rosenzweig, and Levinas proposes it is the core of the Jewish tradition and of humanity as such: substitution and being-for-the-Other. That was also, of course, the intention of Rosenstock-Huessy. It is not by accident that *Practical Knowledge of the Soul* has become part of *Die Sprache des Menschengeschlechts*.

LIFE AND WORK OF
EUGEN ROSENSTOCK-HUESSY

Succinctly we want to give an indication of the place this book occupies in the biography of Rosenstock-Huessy. He was born July 6, 1888, in Berlin into an assimilated Jewish family. His childhood and youth played out in Germany at the end of the nineteenth and the beginning of the twentieth century. He himself says that he understood himself as a Christian from the beginning of his spiritual awakening. There was no sudden conversion. More than once, in that respect, he cited a passage of St. Augustine claiming that the soul is Christian by nature, *naturaliter christiana*. That thought fits nicely into Rosenstock-Huessy's conception of language, in which he argues that we only come to ourselves by an appeal that reaches out to us. This is a Johannine understanding of Christianity, as we have already noted. The "Word" that is from the beginning and that is with God, is of divine origin and calls us into existence. The divine word that calls us to life precedes the independence of the "I". Not paganism, but the love of God is at the origin of humankind.

Recent research has shown that in all probability Eugen Rosenstock-Huessy had decided to be baptized as early as 1906, but according to his recently discovered baptismal certificate he did not take this step until 1909 at age twenty-one. It was a private moment, with no friends or relatives present. Apparently, even the minister who baptized him did not understand the meaning of the text that Rosenstock-Huessy used for baptism, Luke 6:4, as transcribed uniquely in the Codex Bezae: "On that same day he saw somebody working land on the Sabbath, and he said to him: Sir, if you know what you are doing, you are blessed, but if you do not know, you are cursed and an offender of the law". More than once Rosenstock-Huessy referred to that text to emphasize that it is not the act itself but the spirit in which an act is done that is decisive. In that way he understood his belongingness to the Christian tradition. Even more, in that sense he interpreted the core of the Christian tradition!

After his time in a traditional classical gymnasium in Berlin, Rosenstock-Huessy studied the history of law, at Heidelberg University. He graduated there in 1909 at age twenty-one and completed his habilitation in 1912 at the Faculty of Law in Leipzig. He soon got a position there as a *Privatdozent* in the history of medieval law. A *Privatdozent* had the right to lecture at a university, but he was dependent for his income on fees paid by the students attending the lectures. Franz Rosenzweig, although a little older than Rosenstock-Huessy, was among those students, and thus began an intense friendship, cut short by Rosenzweig's early death in 1929.

From his early youth Rosenstock-Huessy had a passionate love for everything related to language. In his book *Ja und Nein, autobiographische Fragmente* (1968) he recounts the large number of projects he was involved in as a teenager and as a schoolboy in relation to language, such as systematically going through etymological dictionaries and translating classical works, among which were Homer and Shakespeare. Besides the compulsory study of language in school, he undertook to learn Egyptian and was able as a fourteen-year-old to translate the Maxims of Ptahhotep. From a very young age, Rosenstock-Huessy saw himself reflected in the words of Johann Georg Hamann "*Sprache ist der Knochen an dem ich ewig nagen werde*" (Language is the bone I shall gnaw on for all eternity).

Rosenstock-Huessy realized that language, speech "das eigentliche Wunder der Wirklichkeit ist" (is the true miracle of reality). Speech binds and changes people. Speech creates exchange and dialogue. By speaking, appealing, and responding a new future emerges. History is created. Language, time, and history in their reciprocal relationships and unity are the great themes that kept Eugen Rosenstock-Huessy occupied all of his life.

During the Great War of 1914-1918, on May 29, 1916, when Rosenzweig was stationed at the Eastern front in the Balkans as a sergeant, and Rosenstock-Huessy was an officer at the Western front in Belgium and France, the correspondence began of which the design of the grammatical method is a part. Following the intensive discussions in 1913, the two men had lost sight of each other for a while. However, in one of the late-night conversations of that earlier time, Rosenstock-Huessy had criticized Rosenzweig for his free-floating Hegelian style of thinking that enabled him to avoid taking a stance on anything. That conversation deeply shocked Rosenzweig, the more so because his fellow intellectual, Rosenstock-Huessy, admitted that for his orientation in the world he relied on prayer in a church. On the verge of converting to Christianity as a remedy for his relativism, Rozenzweig visited a synagogue on Yom Kippur, the Jewish Day of Atonement, and was deeply impressed by the liturgy of this observance, to which

INTRODUCTION

the description in the *Stern* still testifies. Here finally he found the truth for which he could take a stand, and conversion was no more necessary! When Rosenstock-Huessy got the news of Rosenzweig's commitment to Judaism, it prompted the 1916 correspondence, which many years later was published in English as *Judaism Despite Christianity* (1969), edited by Rosenstock-Huessy. In the very last letter of this exchange, Rosenzweig asked Rosenstock-Huessy to write to him "about 'The Languages.'" In response, Rosenstock-Huessy sent him a thirty-page letter that forms the core of *Angewandte Seelenkunde*.

After the First World War, as Rosenstock-Huessy saw it, Germany could not just go on with business as usual. He himself chose not to return to his pre-war existence, and he refused attractive job offers from academe, from government, and from the church. The trial of the war and the collapse of the German Empire reinforced his perception that little was to be expected from the existing institutions, including the universities, to help towards the renewal of man and society. In order to further develop his grammatical method, he was in need of concrete experience that would move in this direction. He offered his services to the auto manufacturer Daimler-Benz and began there the publication of a *Werkzeitung*, the first factory newspaper in Germany, with the intention of starting a dialogue between laborers (18,000 were on strike) and management.

He also had a leadership role in the founding in 1921 of the *Akademie der Arbeit* in Frankfurt, with the same intention of bringing different groups—students, teachers, Communists, socialists, Protestants, Catholics, laborers, jobless people—into dialogue with each other. Some of the *Akademie* staff members, however, had difficulty accepting Rosenstock-Huessy's dialogical concept of "reciprocal learning." The project failed, in particular because his colleagues could not accept that the education of adults is more than just the transfer of knowledge. However, there was a long-term positive resonance from this effort.

In early 1923, with a wife and child to support, Rosenstock-Huessy reluctantly returned to the academy, becoming a professor in the Faculty of Law at the University of Breslau. He looked upon this decision as a defeat, the result of the failure of his initiatives. Nevertheless, from his position at Breslau he later actively participated in the founding of the *Löwenberger Arbeitslager für Arbeiter, Bauern und Studenten* in Silesia. These were work camps for farmers, laborers, and students from all walks of life and different political backgrounds: Communists, (national-) socialists, Catholics, Protestants, Jews, liberals, conservatives, etc. These work camps may be seen as an example of effective adult education.

Within this framework should be mentioned also the meetings some years later at the Von Moltke estate at Kreisau, where during the Second World War representatives of different social groups from Germany secretly discussed the future of a post-Hitler new democratic Germany within the framework of a new democratic Europe. A number of participants in this Kreisau Circle, among them Helmuth James von Moltke, had first become acquainted at the work camps mentioned earlier. By their participation in this Circle they played an important role in the resistance against Hitler and his henchmen, for which Helmuth James paid with his life on Hitler's orders in January 1945. One might say that the Kreisau Circle was the fruit of the labor camps organized with the cooperation of Rosenstock-Huessy in Silesia. For that reason Eugen Rosenstock-Huessy is sometimes called the founding father of the Circle.

In 1933, when the Nazis come to power, Rosenstock-Huessy immediately condemned the new regime as a regression to pre-Christian barbarism. He then and there resigned his professorship at Breslau and arranged to emigrate to the United States. Although as a Jew by birth he would have soon been viciously attacked in Germany, he saw his sudden departure from his home country not only as an escape from the imminent threat of persecution but also as a decisive, principled protest against an evil regime. Through the good offices of a friend at Harvard, Prof. Carl Friedrich, Rosenstock-Huessy had a teaching position waiting for him there, where he remained for a year-and-a-half, subsequently moving to Dartmouth College, in New Hampshire. His teaching at

INTRODUCTION

Dartmouth from 1935 to 1957 inspired a whole generation of students. As a permanent resident in the United States and a citizen after 1944, Rosenstock-Huessy completed the work on his *Soziologie* (Volume I, 1956; Volume II, 1958) and later also his final great work *Die Sprache des Menschengeschlechts* (1963) to which he added at the end of the first volume *Angewandte Seelenkunde* as a compact overview and summary of what he in essence had to say about language. He died at his home in Norwich, Vermont, on February 24, 1973.

THE GRAMMATICAL METHOD

The grammatical method sketched for the first time by Rosenstock-Huessy in *Practical Knowledge of the Soul* is the starting point of his further development as a thinker about language, and it structures all his later work. It will become clear that Rosenstock-Huessy in his grammatical method—also called *"Die höhere Grammatik,"* (the higher grammar) and *"Eine inkarnierende Sprachlehre,"* (an incarnating speech teaching) or also *"Leibhaftige Grammatik"* (incarnated grammar) because we go through the process of change by means of language as living bodies— puts himself at a distance from all philosophical and analytical methods that study words or expressions as part of a language system in the objective sense. On the occasion of the re-publication of *Angewandte Seelenkunde* in *Die Sprache des Menschengeschlechts*, Rosenstock added the following note: "It [the letter to Rosenzweig with Rosenstock's vision of language] went in 1916 as a 'Speech letter' to Franz Rosenzweig in order to *counteract all philosophy of language*, and as such it is the oldest source document of speech thinking in which the era from Parmenides to Hegel is left behind."

With these powerful words Rosenstock-Huessy closed off several thousands of years of language philosophy, but also recounted his own development from an initial passion for philology to a method concerned with living speech. In the end, he looked upon language from a perspective that begins with the origination of man and culminates with the emergence of a peaceful society

Introduction

of the whole human race. For Rosenstock-Huessy, speech is *the shaping and framing power* (*"Sprachkraft"* or *"Nennkraft"*) of human existence. Speech is participation in a world of language from time immemorial; it is earlier than you and more than you. The whole process of being "appealed to," "being named," receiving a first name and responding to it, creates a specific personal room, one's own place and identity in the passage of time. It is a genesis!

In Chapter Five Rosenstock-Huessy speaks of "the grammar of the soul." He poses the question: Does the soul have a grammar? His answer: "Now as the Word comes out of the soul, and the truest Word comes straight from the very depths of the soul; and since we measure the power of speech precisely by its impact on the soul, . . . then, just as the mind has logic, the soul will have a sense of the way words fit together as its inner structure—that is, grammar . . . . The programmatic character of this essay therefore cannot be anything other than *grammatical* . . . . Grammar is the key that unlocks the door to the soul. He who would explore the soul must fathom the secrets of language."

Precisely that is the program of this small book. The secrets of language are methodically revealed, bit by bit. First and very powerfully this takes place by the denunciation of the Greek or Alexandrian grammar table, which for centuries has been compulsory language drilling for students, the familiar verb conjugation beginning "I love," "you love," "s/he loves," etc. We are all contaminated by it unto the depths of our souls. "I" in this ancient structure is the first person, but no one before Rosenstock-Huessy questioned whether this honored place is in agreement with the reality of our grammatical experiences. Yet, as Rosenstock-Huessy points out, it is only by means of the name by which the newborn child is addressed that he or she is incorporated into the world of language from time immemorial— *"you* are loved, John." It takes a while before the child discovers himself as an "I", a subject. The child is incorporated into language, language being, Rosenstock argues, "wiser than the one who speaks it." The human being, the child, from the beginning is approachable by speech. He is callable; he can be appealed to. He can be addressed by his name. The

INTRODUCTION

child is therefore not an "I" in the first place but a "you" or a "thou." It is from this "being called by one's name" that the grammatical method takes its point of departure. The starting point is being "spoken to."

Technically we are referring to the vocative mood. The vocative mood is the address or the appeal, which always comes first—"You, Mary." It precedes all other speech, not only biographically from birth but also throughout life. Being named puts people on the move, makes them stand up and go. Directly related to the vocative mood and combined with it, is the imperative (compare the "command" in Rosenzweig and Levinas). The imperative mood is the most original form of the verb and the shortest form: Laugh! Walk! Look! Wait! Stand up! Go! Only the root of the verb is used, which feeds the presumption that all other forms of the verb are derived from it. However, the imperative is not by itself a complete sentence. It bridges the distance between the speaker and the listener and implies and evokes an answer, a response. Will that answer follow? The listener always has a choice between "yes" and "no." "Will you follow"? "Yes, I will follow." The one who says "yes, I follow," the addressee, provides the subject for which the verb in the imperative mood is searching. With the imperative, something is going to happen. The situation is going to change. A process of change is initiated. The imperative mood is challenging and for that reason it is called the "mode of change." Change and renewal is what Rosenstock-Huessy's grammar of the soul envisions, and therefore it can also be called "the doctrine of transformative change." One thinks here of Rosenstock-Huessy's credo: *Respondeo etsi mutabor* —I respond although I will be changed in the process.

In this brief introduction there is space only to cite these two first principles of the "*Leibhaftige Gammatik*": the "you" comes before the "I", and the *change* that the vocative mood and the imperative mood effectuate. These are the first steps towards the grammatical method that is presented in *Practical Knowledge of the Soul*. This grammar comprises the miracle of becoming human. We must, however, pay attention, too, to the other term in the title, "soul." A person searching for a convincing definition of the soul will give up after a while, with some disappointment. The meaning of "soul" cannot be pinned down in a fixed formula. Nevertheless, as Rosenstock-Huessy asserts, there is a deep longing to unravel the secrets of the soul. In our time the term emerges rather often, maybe because people feel that the predominant scientific and objectifying understanding of mind and body does not touch the secret of being human.

Immediately the question is raised in this book whether "practical knowledge of the soul" is the same as "practical psychology." The question needs an answer. What does the word "psyche" mean and what do we understand by "soul"? Rosenstock-Huessy pays a lot of attention to the difference between the two. The word "soul" evokes all sorts of memories, thoughts, and subjects that we do not connect with the word "psyche." But what then is the content of the word "soul"? First Rosenstock-Huessy answers negatively with a short and powerful statement: The soul is not a thing. But what is the soul?

We already heard the statement of Rosenstock-Huessy: "Just as the mind has logic, the soul will have a sense of the way words fit together as its inner structure—that is, grammar." That means, in the search for the soul Rosenstock-Huessy discovered a structure of language, the source of language, the primary grammar, the starting point of the power of speech. One might say this is the result of the search: The rediscovery of language as the power of speech, in which the vocative mood and the imperative mood constantly initiate change and renewal of man and society. One might then say: The soul is that in human beings that reveals and leads the process of change. Change occurs when a new love enters, a new command, a new imperative. That in us from which love springs, our passion, or whatever one is inclined to call it, that is our soul. At the same time, we are not fully conscious of this loving capacity for change that lives in us. One might also say: The soul is that part of our heart that loves, but without our being in control and fully conscious of that love. The soul is that power in us that is beyond ourselves, and that leads to the unknown future.

Introduction

It is that part of us that is already on the other side, and our mind and body cannot do otherwise but follow suit.

THE GRAMMATICAL METHOD IN THE FURTHER WORK OF ROSENSTOCK-HUESSY

How is the grammatical method applied in the further work of Rosenstock-Huessy? We want to value this method for what it is worth, indicate the importance of it in the "genesis" of the neighbor, of human beings, of a people, of Europe, of the world. That is quite a claim, but that is what the grammatical method promises.

Chapter Ten of *Practical Knowledge of the Soul*, with the title "Our People," suggests a grammatical model that Rosenstock-Huessy applies to history. The result is his comprehensive language-historical book *Die Europäischen Revolutionen und der Charakter der Nationen*, published in 1931. As stated above, in 1938, expanded with new material and a different chronological order, it was published in English under the title *Out of Revolution: Autobiography of Western Man*. Indeed it contains an "autobiography of Western man" because it not only presents facts but focuses on the events that made us what we are. These are truly events. Only when we are fundamentally changed by history can a happening really count as an event. These events are connected to the new imperatives that emerge and are articulated from time to time in history. In response to these imperatives, people take daring new steps resulting in the framing and shaping of new institutions. Each of the great European revolutions created a new human type with new qualities, new laws, and new forms of language.

The grammatical method is also the foundation of Rosenstock-Huessy's encompassing language-sociology, entitled *Soziologie* (1956-58). In two big volumes he goes through all world history. Each phase in history is characterized by a new "way of speech." Again, these new forms of speech that organize a society emerged as a response to the urgently felt needs of the time. For instance, the ancient Egyptian empire is a response to the need and the chaos of the tribes before that time, their struggle for life

INTRODUCTION

in that fertile land. Ancient Israel and Greece can as well be understood as a reaction to the hierarchical harness that this imperial culture, by its strict organization, imposed on its subjects. Israel brought about a rupture with the cyclical, Egyptian hierarchical order by prioritizing a future of justice above the existing earthly order. The God of Israel is coming from the future and justice is preparing his way (Psalm 85:14). Greece softened this hierarchical order, in Homer, in the tragedies, and in philosophy by sympathizing with the tragic human being who cannot escape the laws of the cosmos. In each new way of speech social reality is ordered and arranged anew.

The final application of this method is in Rosenstock-Huessy's third great work, *Die Sprache des Menschengeschlechts* (1963). The institutions realized in the course of history are crystallizations of new ways of speech, which have been revealed to and discovered by man in the course of history. Thereby the human race is constantly enriched by ever-new forms and expressions of speech. In this way the creation of God progresses towards its fulfillment. The vast language repertoire at the disposal of the human race increases in the course of history on the condition that being human means remaining flexible, receptive, moldable, and open to the future. The importance of this plasticity was once more emphasized by Rosenstock-Huessy when he put at the end of *Die Sprache des Menschengeschlechts* a work entitled *Die Frucht der Lippen* (Fruit of Lips) about the four Gospels, in which he shows how Jesus Christ bestowed this transformative power on the entire human race.

OVERVIEW AND STRUCTURE OF *PRACTICAL KNOWLEDGE OF THE SOUL*

The work before you has twelve chapters which can be grouped in three sections of four each. In the first group of four chapters Rosenstock-Huessy clears the way for his conception of language and the soul. He points to the weak spot in the existing theories and shows why a new understanding of language and soul is necessary and possible. The next four chapters provide the core of the

INTRODUCTION

new teaching. This approach to language was devised by a group of friends in the crisis of the First World War as the outcome of a revelatory experience. The final four chapters of the book explore the consequences of this new discovery in relation to the dominant conceptions of language and the soul, and show the application of the method to the usual disciplines and to the life of the nation. There the new approach is put into practice and realized.

With this threefold structure it immediately becomes clear that this new conception of language is presented in a trinitarian rhythm: Creation – Revelation – Redemption. Creation: the present situation shows a deadlock or a lacuna. Revelation: a new inspiration and command opens hitherto untrodden roads. Redemption: following those roads creates new institutions and a new world. But after some time these new institutions end up in a deadlock and ossify, and once more a new revelation is needed. In that fashion, the history of salvation moves forward. The *Stern* of Rosenzweig shows the same threefold structure. That is not to say that Rosenzweig's plan came only from Rosenstock-Huessy's 1916 letter, but that both friends had a common horizon arising from their many discussions.

Each of the three sections in *Practical Knowledge of the Soul* is divided into four chapters, as noted. The chapters follow the structure of the "cross of reality," as Rosenstock-Huessy likes to call the intersecting space and time vectors—inside and outside, future and past. Life, reality, constantly pulls us in four different directions. Regularly, in one order or the other, an event may be described from four different angles: the origin or the past; the change or the future; the subjective feeling at the inner pole; and the objective facts at the outside. Below, we indicate that structure in our short reading guide.

INTRODUCTION

1. The present course of events: Creation

Chapter One: Is Seelenkunde *the same as practical psychology?*

German language purists started to use the word *Seelenkunde* for psychology, appropriating the noun for soul, "Seele." That may seem to be a superficial change, but, following Rosenstock-Huessy, it has enormous consequences for the connotations and meanings its evokes. The word "soul" has a peculiar resonance in our inner life. At the beginning the introduction of a new word seems only something incidental, on the surface. But the translation of "psychology" as *Seelenkunde* evokes meanings that lie deeper. (Here we see *the outside objective pole of the cross*).

Chapter Two: Psychology as a science

In philosophy and science, soul and mind are often identified (if the word "soul" is invoked at all) as though there is no difference. Mind usually means: our thinking or the subjective point of view. Science approaches the soul in this way, from the inside, as a subject. At most, science will admit that there is something more going on, which requires applying a holistic method (psychosomatic). (Here is the *inside subjective pole of the cross*).

Chapter Three: The psyche

The psyche seen as a transformer of physical data or as a receiving terminal of spiritual data is described by Rosenstock-Huessy as a problem not responded to and not solved. How are mind and body related in the life of the psyche? This question is usually avoided, just as a responsibility or a new imperative may be avoided. The magic word "psychosomatic" is supposed to do the job. But that does not explain anything. In this way Rosenstock-Huessy points to the weak spot, the lacuna, which should lead to a change of the dominant theoretical approach. (This is *the future "prejective" pole in the cross*).

Chapter Four: The occult sciences

In the occult sciences we encounter a tradition that tries to fill this lacuna, providing a solution regarding the "psyche," but it is one-sided. We are, according to the premises of occult science, linked to matter, fused together with it in our becoming. In that respect, occult science has a point, but the solution it proposes tells only half of the story. The soul is now understood as a power in the world, a special sort of magical force in nature. In this way occult science actually leaves the lacuna unfilled. (This is *the past "trajective" pole of the cross*).

2. The Change: Revelation

Chapter Five: The grammar of the soul

Both individual and community undergo a process of change, from 'you', to 'I', to 'we', to 'it'. It all begins with the imperative, the future (*the future pole of the cross*).

Chapter Six: The destination of the soul

The meaning of "soul" for every human being encompasses a special and separate history, a distinct biography, a whole integrated life from birth to death. By this definition, the grammatical method answers a question that is left aside by psychology and that occult science answers in a misleading way (*the past pole of the cross*).

Chapter Seven: The powers of the soul

Here the focus is on the inside, on the subjective. But the subject is not the source of an initiative but rather the addressee of an imperative, a "you" or "thou" from whom a response is expected. Mustering courage and enduring fear are the powers that bridge the abyss of the crisis (*the inside pole in the cross of reality*).

Chapter Eight: Community

If more than one person becomes involved in the process of change (because individual souls succeed in overcoming shame and fear, and come forward to help each other in some sort of division of labor), an effective community comes into being in the outside world, with the result that the change becomes institutionalized and thereby irreversible (*outside pole of the cross*).

3. Realization: Redemption

Chapter Nine: The language of the community

The traditional division of disciplines, such as art, science, religion, etc., is given a new interpretation by Rosenstock-Huessy that puts the disciplines within the framework of the grammatical method. What in Chapter Five was described with a flash of new insight is here methodically exposed in all its consequences (*the outside pole*).

Chapter Ten: Our people

Following this methodological exposition, attention is focused once more on the challenge faced by this method. Can it offer those who have lost their soul a new inspiration and heal them (*the future pole of the cross*)?

Chapter Eleven: Spirit, soul, and body

The traditional partition between soul and body, which leads to fragmentation, is replaced by the tri-partition of spirit, soul, and body, in which it is the soul that creates unity and points the way forward. The soul is ahead of mind and body. In this way a new subject, moving from "you" to "I", is called into being. Both mind and body are pulled forward by the transformation of the soul that follows the command (*inside pole*).

Introduction

Chapter Twelve: The grammatical method

Now we can look back and mark the road that leads from scholasticism (Middle Ages) via the sciences (modernity) towards the new method, the grammatical method. In this way the grammatical method receives its due place in the historical progress of the human race (*the past pole*).

It is our hope that by means of this short introduction, the reader has gained some insight into the fundamental importance of this book that aims to bring about a "Copernican revolution" in our thinking, speaking, and acting, degenerated though they have been by the grammatical system inherited from the Greeks.

Hans van der Heiden
Otto Kroesen
Henk van Olst

1

Practical Study of the Soul

WHENEVER GERMAN PATRIOTISM HEATS up, there is a sharp increase in the tendency to "Germanize" foreign words. Supposedly having many foreign words makes it difficult for the masses to enter the halls of knowledge, and the masses are what publishers, politicians, and adult-education teachers want to reach. So all these "evil" foreign words are being translated. In store windows today you can see books entitled, "A Primer on Health" instead of "Hygiene"; "A Primer on Society" instead of "Sociology"; and "A Primer on Stars" instead of "Astronomy." Nevertheless, if you open these books, you will find that they still contain traditional academic and professional organization of material, train of thought, and presentation of argument. Only the title itself has really been translated.

Even so, "mere" names contain a power that goes beyond the intention of their authors or speakers. For names contain spirit. The author of a new name will soon have to confess, "The spirits that I have summoned I can no longer get rid of" [Goethe, *Der Zauberlehrling*]. "A Primer on Stars" will never again be familiar old "Astronomy." New names have a way of leading to new thoughts, even if the author chose an everyday title without thinking much about it, following the advice of the community college's Dean of the Faculty, or of his publisher, or of the German Language Association. These new thoughts, however, will not at first occur to the innocent specialist himself, but rather to one who listens or reads faithfully.

Each new name is actually a double-edged sword, only one edge of which is under the control of the author and the traditions of his scientific discipline. The effects of the other edge are determined by the people to whom the specialists have unwittingly handed the new name, not by the specialists themselves. Had they continued to use a technical, esoteric term, this wouldn't have happened. Esoteric terms are puzzling labels for strange subject matter. Anyone buying the label also has to put up with letting the specialists—the experts who control these esoteric words—have the authority to define the content of the strange subject matter. But this stops being true as soon as people's everyday language takes over a subject matter. Then the reader, summoned and seduced by its new name, is free willfully to apply adjectives and pronouns to the subject.

The esoteric discipline will be most thoroughly transformed when the new name is truly a well-known name, which resonates off the everyday experiences of a people. If you call an automobile a "car" (which comes from carriage), you make it a more popular thing, because the city dwellers and the farmers may have already owned carriages. However, if you translate "sociology" as "a primer on society," you don't accomplish much, because people are more familiar with social issues than with primers and theories. The term "sociology" won't begin to resonate in people until it can be called "a primer on people." That speaks to everybody.

However, it is the science of psychology which today already arouses a thousand-fold echo—sympathetic as well as antagonistic. Its name will have been put into everyday language before that of sociology. Psychology has been the preserve of philosophers and the philosophically educated for a long time. They have seen it as a fashionable sideline to their education, because psycho-babble appeals to women in fashionable society. Today, however, psychology is becoming practical. There is already a journal called "Practical

Psychology." This means that psychology is leaving the narrow circle of the philosophical world and attempting to become accessible to everybody, even while remaining every inch a science.

Psychologists are starting to work in the fields of politics, education, and economics. They are developing psychology of advertising, "psycho-technology," and child psychology. They are dissecting the sense of shame, and this anatomical approach is quickly becoming famous as psychoanalysis. They conduct tests on hundreds of school children, selecting the talented ones. They have come up with mass psychology to explain mass demonstrations and demagogues. They offer psychotherapies. In the light of this rich harvest of developments, it's fitting that psychologists feel the need to communicate their work to a wide circle. The industrial workers, who are the subjects of psycho-technical testing and evaluation, should be able to find out what their "psyches" really are. And so it is not surprising that many pamphlets and adult education courses are addressing themselves to this issue.

Considering all this, we are honor-bound to translate the esoteric words into everyday language. And, lo and behold, "practical psychology" [in German] turns into practical study of the soul [*angewandte Seelenkunde*]. It's true that the layman runs out of patience and curiosity when confronted by the word "psycho-technology." But the new name, "practical study of the soul," calls his whole heritage of belief and tradition into play. Soul: everybody already knows something about the soul. It's just that everybody thinks this topic belongs in Sunday school, meaning our involvement with it should stop at age fourteen.

Dear Soul, now the adults are suddenly encountering you again, this time as a scientific fact or even as a discovery.

People who take seriously battles over philosophies of life or views of the world [*Weltanschauung*] are especially likely to be interested in pursuing the riddles of the soul. So they will check out the community college, looking for discoveries about the soul itself. But they will find the instructor has done nothing beyond re-baptizing and watering down "practical psychology" into "practical study of the soul." And neither re-baptizing nor watering down accomplishes anything. So a chasm is opening up between the esoteric subject matter and the popular name. The reader can see how deep this chasm is by looking at William James (1842-1910), the greatest American psychologist. He specifically rejected the idea of using the word "soul" anywhere in his widely read work, *Psychology*. He said he found absolutely no occasion to use it. So isn't it deceptive to translate the word "psychology" into "knowledge of the soul"?

2

The Science of Psychology

As we said, a practical study of the soul sells the same bill of goods as so-called practical psychology. It differs only in name from the science that is being taught nowadays and whose technique is being applied at institutions of higher learning. It would lead too far afield to provide a history of the discipline here. In any case, the field is constantly expanding, for instance into animal psychology (smart Hans, the apes of Tenerife, etc.). Nor is providing a history necessary in view of the double-edged nature of new names, bestowed by authors largely unaware of what they are doing. Nevertheless, as we have already admitted, only part of the effect is unknown to the author. The rest remains, undisturbed, the concern of the particular professional field, staying in the laboratory, the test station, the seminar, and the classroom.

We, however, are interested only in the conflict between the new name, "a practical study of the soul," and the old, age-old, reality of the soul. And in this context, we aren't exaggerating when we say that a person taking in a lecture on "applied study of the soul" at a community college would not be interested in discourses on intelligence tests, controlled experiments, touch and pressure sensation, illusions, and suggestions. The poor listener would respond to these discourses as he would to those of most other scientific disciplines. He would be deeply disappointed that attractive titles should conceal such banal content. Many listeners might not even admit this disappointment to themselves. But practical psychology would have failed to meet their expectations. The urge that had made them come had sprung from something more vital and important, a mixture of curiosity, longing, and awe regarding the secrets of the soul.

The scientific literature talks about these secrets of the soul only in a negative way, namely, when the author defines the limits of his field. This is a kind of negative knowledge of the soul based on the model of negative theology. There, people often say: God, in any case, is not the way you imagine Him to be. Similarly, people often say: The soul, in any case, is not what scientists imagine it to be. This is a step in the right direction. It is undoubtedly true that psychology today has basically nothing to do with the secrets of the soul.

But we have to go further and make the positive assertion that psychologists concern themselves only with two facades of the soul, rather than dealing in any way with the whole sphere of the soul itself. The two outer sides of the soul face the physical and mental aspects of life. We find that modern psychologists thoroughly investigate physical facets (senses, reactions) and mental facets (memory and intelligence), studying impressions and traces of the physical and conceptual worlds. This has serious consequences. Seen this way, the psychological sphere is nothing but a ball tossed between the output of the physical and the output of the mental aspects of life. Some think it belongs to the realm of the material while others think it belongs to the realm of the spiritual; at times it is understood as an antenna for signals from the body, at times as memory and as a processor for ideas. Different schools of thought selectively mix and combine that extremely materialistic concept of the psyche with that extremely idealistic one. A valid example of this can be found in a scholarly book that appeared after 1900 and enjoyed a second edition and hence, success. It was thoroughly professional and scientific, including the most up-to-date research. The book is hundreds of pages long and entitled *Geist und Körper, Seele und Leib* [Mind and Body, Soul and Physique]. The title doesn't refer to four different concepts. As he shows by using "body" and "physique," the author doesn't think he is talking about four different things, but rather that "mind" and "soul" are just as identical as "body" and "physique" are. He recognizes one dichotomy only: mind versus nature. And he wants to express each of the antithetical poles in a two-fold way. Fascinated by the dichotomy, mind and soul versus body and physique, the book does not even raise the *question* of whether mind and soul are identical. For academic philosophy, this question simply doesn't arise.

But we have a thousand reasons to be thoroughly suspicious of any disembodying of the mind or "de-mentalizing" of the body. We find it more likely that body and mind are different facets of the same order of things. So it would seem that both parties are wrong in the whole battle between idealism and materialism, and in the battle between the "monism" of the materialists and the "dualism" of the idealists as well. Neither philosophers nor their opponents have an inkling of the truly crucial dichotomy, although the philosopher naively preserved it in the title "Mind and Body, Soul and Physique." The language which offered him two words, "mind" and "soul," tricked him and proved to be smarter than he, the alleged interpreter.

Incidentally, it would be unjust not to admit that academic philosophy has already made large concessions to the powerful process by which philosophy's old problems disappear and are replaced by new ones. Under the impact of a kind of dead-end situation or a bankruptcy of the professional language of psychology, Wertheimer, Goldstein, Gelb, Koffka, Adler, and others have started taking account of everyday life.[1] These researchers also submit the psychological sphere to procedures appropriate to the physical and the mental spheres, but they emphasize strongly that we ought to use the so-called holistic method when we study the

---

1. Max Wertheimer, Kurt Goldstein, Adhémar Gelb, Kurt Koffka, Alfred Adler were all figures associated with the Gestalt school of psychology and roughly contemporary in age with Rosenstock-Huessy.

soul, because the soul is a unique, all-embracing process to which all individual processes ought to be related.

Academic scientists cannot really turn their backs on the physiological-spiritual dilemma, which for the last sixty years has been referred to by the completely misleading name of the psycho-physical "connection" or "dichotomy". Professional psychologists can't turn their backs on it either and still remain within the accepted research standpoint, which is rooted in dualistic academic science and ultimately in idealism. Professional psychologists still consider it an immense achievement if they treat only half of the soul as if it were merely the mind.

Theodor Erismann's book *Die Eigenart des Geistigen, Induktive und einsichtige Psychologie* (1924) [The Idiosyncrasy of Things Mental: Inductive and Intuitive Psychology] is the latest example of an academic approach helplessly trapped between nature and mind like a donkey between two bundles of hay. Even in the title he confuses "mental" research with research into the soul, and it gets worse in the body of the book. This work is typical of hundreds like it.

3

The Psyche

WHEN WE HEAR OF "practical study of the soul," however, we think neither of sensory functions nor of output of the mind (these are things the soul uses), but of a third distinct reality. The classical expression "psyche" does not fit this reality exactly. Rather here we really need the German word "*Seele*," just as the French would have to speak of "*âme*," and the English of "soul" and not of "*psychologie*" [French] and "psychology"[English]. The expression "psyche" has the connotation of the soul in a certain condition. It describes a discernible and confirmable "moment of the soul" or "state of the soul," a soul wedged between bodily and mental influences. So it's proper for a physician to speak of the psyche of his patient. Being concerned first with the body, a physician will notice that aspect of a person's psychological makeup that accompanies his illness. Whether the physician's attention lasts fourteen days or two years, it is drawn to the psyche by the state of the body. This state is nearly always short-lived in comparison to the total life span of the patient, and so the physician's interest remains fragmentary.

Scholars, humanists, teachers, and so forth, also have reason to speak of the "psyche" of the individual. But they do so from a different standpoint. The behavior of parts of the body pointed the physician to the background: psyche. In the case of the scholars, etc., the whole mental world of the *"logos"* is the observer's point of view. Coming from the realm of ideas, he is amazed at the ability of the poor little individual psyche to comprehend all the fields of knowledge, as well as to make moral and aesthetic judgments. The whole spiritual realm descends as tradition, education, teaching, morals, imitation, and more, and penetrates each individual. The psyche is capable of absorbing universal things like these. We study the psyche because it is remarkable and impressive that the spirit, which is universal, descends again and again into thousands of individuals.

For someone whose points of reference are ideas and the life of the mind, the psyche is primarily the universal concept for a more or less capable "transformer," which is what each man represents as he receives the infinite streams of the spirit. So his will, intelligence, and emotional life are examined. No wonder, then, that the research criteria applied to the part of the soul involved with the intellect are primarily *speed* of comprehension and ability to save time. For the intellect is outside time. Therefore, it is easy to make the mistake of assuming that the faster the psyche, the more mentally competent it must be. Under "psyche" today we understand a place where we respond to physical reality or receive spiritual reality. These two aspects of the soul are the subject matter of modern scientific psychology.

We cannot be satisfied with this duality, since the psychologists themselves are already aware of a third area, the "psychic," existing between the first two. But they understandably avoid this area like the plague. One might even say that psychology as a science owes its formation to the fact that the intellect has fled from this uncanny middle region. The modern psychologist dares to approach this domain only from the outside and then he walls it off with a high fence as if it were a dangerous fault in a region full of mine shafts. We have in mind here the type of psyche which is the subject matter of the occult sciences. Regarding these areas of the soul, it is customary to refer to Max Dessoirs's book, *Vom Jenseits der Seele* (1920) [From Beyond the Soul] which, in order to remain scientific, remains purely descriptive. That way, you can stay as pure as the driven snow. You haven't compromised yourself. You remain objective. The "beyond" really lies beyond; and consequently this kind of psyche lies beyond the realm of science.

But this simple word "beyond" needs some clarification. If the occult sciences (theosophy, spiritualism, astrology, and the like) are of no use in researching the human psyche, it's not because official science has completely and satisfactorily asked the right questions. In fact, contemporary science fails us in this regard. Occult science fails also, but at least it does ask the right questions. Its failure lies elsewhere and, strangely enough, even its enemies don't bring it up. We will have to touch upon this briefly in order to justify our opposition both to the occult sciences and to scientific psychology.

4

The Occult Sciences

THE OCCULT "SCIENCES" PRESERVE for mankind knowledge of the cosmic powers of the human soul. Just as the cabalists wanted to dissolve Christ into a purely tellural transformation process of creation, theosophists strive to understand the individual person as a natural power, a demon or an emergent form of nature. In its ascent (purification) or in its migration (transmigration of the soul!), the form has the power to carry along with it other creatures or natural substances, and to recreate and develop them. Magic, telepathy, spiritualism, and hypnosis concern themselves with the human soul as a ruling or yielding power in the world.

Let's take prophecy, a central concern, in which we can trace the mundane roots of these excessively fantastic schools of thought. Either there is a power that can take hold of a single person, allowing people suddenly to be able to read in him the laws of the world and human history as if he were an open book, or belief in revelation of any kind—that is, all the religion in the old and new covenant—is a swindle. Psychologists cannot claim to be innocent of this and say, as they like to do, that this is not one of their concerns, and that it belongs to the province of theologians.

At this point, it's untenable to divide the truth into two parts, for prophecy is a *natural* disposition of the soul, a disposition that must be present already so that a subsequent understanding of God or history or nature may enter a soul. Theologians can only distinguish between true and false prophets, between Moses and the magicians of the pharaoh, or between Paul and Simon the magician, or between Swedenborg and [Johann Georg] Hamann, if they can and may pre-suppose the general faculty of prophecy within the realm of the soul.[1] The soul either can conduct the streams of the spirit or it cannot. These powers of the soul should be investigated in terms of human, not supernatural, experience.

This is a very sober and everyday affair. Just as rats desert a sinking ship, so living people smell misfortunes or fortune every day. The saying about the rats shows how natural we think this is. Prophecy and magic merely demonstrate man's embeddedness in creation in a gigantic way. Our innate embeddedness can reach either far into time (prophecy) or dramatically through space (magic). We might call prophecy an uncanny embeddedness in world history, while we might call magic a dramatic embeddedness into the cosmic universe, the contemporary universe.

Today books are dealing again with prophetic socialism, magic religion, prophetic romanticism, mysticism, etc., and this jargon reveals how people are recognizing again, often perhaps in an unpleasant way, that the soul is embedded in the world. If we deny this, as people did in the nineteenth century, we immediately transform history and order into historical rubble and delusion.

Jesus, for instance, would have been nothing but a fanatic dreamer had He not carried within His own soul the full time span from Adam and Moses to Himself. Only because He did was He later accorded a corresponding power to shape the future. That power reaches from Him—through the Church and Christendom—to the end of the world, and is undeniably still being revealed to us every day since we are still fighting about Him as much as ever before.

1. Rosenstock-Huessy seems to have lost the parallelism of his examples here. One would expect Moses, Paul, and Hamann to be on one side, and the pharaoh's magicians, Simon the magus, and Swedenborg to be on the other. Hamann, whom Rosenstock-Huessy greatly respected, and Swedenborg got switched.

By not recognizing these powers as important predispositions of the everyday life of the soul, psychologists are robbing of their natural fertile soil (the only place they become imaginable or believable) the few outstanding people who reconcile and connect the ages of world history. By not taking a stand of their own, psychologists seem to allow theologians to promote an exaggerated cult of religious hero-worship. In reality, however, psychologists ridicule all theology.

Religious teachers are indeed undertaking an impossible task when they attribute certain characteristics and abilities to only a handful of individuals—characteristics not to be found in others, either in the bud or as perversions. Theologians do in fact suffer from this state of affairs, and so have already developed the special discipline of "religious psychology" (James; Wobbermin).[2] But this inevitably turns into a mere "religious pathology" because they are forced to treat a potentially higher story of the soul—the religious domain—without its natural ground floor. While we can find an abundance of religious delusions and philistinisms in James, sound living faith is missing and has to be, because all standards of health and naturalness disappear as soon as this realm of the soul is no longer considered an obvious endowment of every human soul.

This is the natural foundation on which all faith rests, and the occult sciences preserve it. And that is why to this day they have proved ineradicable. The uselessness of their results must be caused by something other than the wrong choice of topics. It is not the senseless topics, but the wrong methods that have led to arbitrary results. This mistake in choosing the method is the same mistake scientific psychologists make! It's just that the mistake comes home to roost much more obviously in the case of the occult teachings; so it is important to articulate the mistake clearly.

What's so frightening about the occult sciences? They claim that any being, i.e., an individual soul, can exert a power over the world or over the immediate environment; a soul can train itself

---

2. William James, not really a theologian but certainly a student of religious psychology, and Georg Wobbermin, d. 1943, a Lutheran theologian in Germany who translated James's *Varieties of Religious Experience* into German.

(yoga) to master cunning abilities; it can call up spirits and phenomena. But these souls are individual, independent molecules in the universe, every being is the bearer of a separate consciousness, each "having it out with the world," as people so nicely put it.[3] Now we suspect that the order of the world would collapse if this were so. And we are right. A world consisting of just many isolated beings would be tolerable only as long as these beings were harmless pedestrians. But if every individual could mobilize cosmic powers, if everyone could set heaven or hell in motion, then this world would destroy itself in spasms and explosions. Basically, every honest person knows that the teachings of the spiritualists, etc., are lies—and knows it for reasons that are much better than mere theories. Self-preservation and the preservation of the species make it obvious that the devil is at work here. But that's just what makes occultism exciting and attractive. Theoretical arguments against it simply miss the point.

Psychologists, too, assume that there are only lots of individual beings! Of course, philosophical psychologists remain faithful to the rationalistic principle of all philosophy by beginning with the "I", the single rational ego, instead of beginning with a "being," as do those who believe in the magical world. Both reduce the soul to a single shape only. The psychologists also claim that the "I" is always coming to terms with the various "things" in the outer and inner world: with the objects of nature (sensory and perceptual psychology), with society (social psychology), with the treasures of the mind [*Geistesleben*], and finally, with itself or even with God.

The philosopher however, considers this "I", the "subject" of a philosophy of life, to be a very powerless being, "objectively" speaking. His "I" isn't as dangerous as the "being" of an occultist. A doubting and discerning thinker's "I" is purely inward-oriented, mental, and reasonable; so it doesn't burst into reality with omnipotent destructive gestures. However, the "psyche" of philosophy, as well as that of occultism, has been ripped out of the circuit that

---

3. German: "*sich mit der Welt auseinandersetzt*," a play on words meaning, idiomatically, arguing with the world and literally separating itself from the world.

switched it between God and the world, and lies isolated under glass. Still, the psyche carries with it into isolation something that it doesn't have in occultism: namely, its reasonableness. A philosopher's "I"s are souls addressed as reasonable souls, who in exchange have lost all power over the world. But in their power over truth, they are like God. All that is left of the world is a semblance of beauty which the "I" cannot even take for itself but which, at best, is given. The German Platonists are the main exponents of this theory. After all, Plato is the quintessential philosophical type.

We can now summarize. The philosopher's mistake is that while his "I"s are divine by virtue of their possession of reason, they are powerless shadows in the face of the laws of the world. The occultist's mistake is that while his "soul-beings" are endowed with all the powers of the world, they forfeit their share of divine reason. A philosopher's "I"s are mental giants; an occultist's "mediums" are cosmic giants. On the one hand, the soul is a thoroughly reasonable personality; on the other, it's a cosmic force of monstrous capability which can conjure up whole worlds and make them disappear before our eyes.

We are at the roots of two age-old, eternal, ineradicable eccentricities of human nature: Orient and Occident, yoga and philosophy, asceticism of the body and "logicism" of the mind. These are the one-sided extremes which mankind embraces daily to avoid the balance provided by its soul. Orient and Occident, monks and academics, Buddha and Plato tyrannize the soul. I quote: "the soul is not a thing." Both mistakes can be traced to the same error. They apply a false grammar to the soul, or more precisely, they employ an impoverished grammar. And the psyche thus scourged has to fight off academic specialists and occultists by consoling itself with the words of the poet:

> Soll dich der Olymp begrüssen
> arme Psyche, musst Du büssen.
> Eros, der dich sucht und peinigt,
> will dich seelig und gereinigt.

> If Olympus is to greet you
> Poor Psyche, you must do penance.
> Eros, who is looking for and torturing you,
> Wants you redeemed and purified.

We, however, are looking for Eros himself instead of those instruments of torture.

5

The Grammar of the Soul

Does the soul have a grammar? Now as the Word comes out of the soul, and the truest Word comes straight from the very depths of the soul; and since we measure the power of speech precisely by its impact on the soul, when (as the poet says)

> des Sängers Lied aus dem Innern schallt
> und wecket der dunkeln Töne Gewalt,
> die im Herzen wunderbar schliefen
>
> The singer's song sounds from within
> And awakens the power of dark sounds
> Which slept wondrously in the heart,

then, just as the mind has logic, the soul will have a sense of the way words fit together as its inner structure—that is, "grammar." This analogy is not to be taken lightly, but is meant rather in *all* of its apprehendable import. The programmatic character of this essay therefore cannot be anything other than *grammatical*. While logic and the theory of cognition constitute the core of all the humanities, while natural sciences rise and fall with mathematics, grammar is the key that unlocks the door to the soul. He who would explore the soul must fathom the secrets of language. But is there a mere scholar (other than a born—by the grace of God—psychologist) who knows this? Is there an occultist who does? Quite the contrary, both practically avoid and flee this effective method of understanding the soul.

The philosopher wants to reach the soul logically, with epistemological presuppositions. His method of approaching the soul is as flawed as the medieval scholastic's method of approaching nature. Even today all of the humanities amount to unproven scholasticism when touching on questions of the soul, as in law, economics, history, and above all, in psychology. If we want to grasp the present state of official science of the soul, we should think of natural science before mathematics and experimentation liberated it from the tyranny of logic.

On the other hand, the occultists, the monists, and their ilk want to master the soul by using precisely these modern methods. So they approach the soul with calculations that are more or less (mostly less) modern, but that are, in any case, based on space and nature, or astrology and mathematics. These thinkers always have to "materialize" the soul. To them, the highest revelations of the soul are processes of materialization and experiments by mediums. This is just as perverse and, in terms of the soul, obscene as the philosopher's declaration that its innermost secret is rationality.

Academic psychologists claim that the "I" is the sole absolute. The "you", the "he", the "she", the "it" of things—everything else—is noteworthy only when it is taken up by this grammatical first person, by this "I" within the soul. The "I" classifies "non-I"s, or its brothers, or God, or other objects. This view corresponds to the assertion of Greek grammarians that the "I" is the first person of the verb. So we can see clearly that it originated from an antiquated—Spengler would say Euclidian—standpoint of thinking. Nowadays, Greek philosophy and Greek academic grammar are no longer a valid basis for such far-reaching assertions. The "I" may still be called the first person in our textbooks, but psychologists may no longer naively accept this incorrect enumeration as dogma. For all of our own experience teaches us exactly the opposite of this Greek premise, that the single "I" is primary.

Out of a thousand cares, impressions, and influences that surround, flow around, and beset it, a child gradually stakes out its borders as an independent entity. Its first discovery on its own, therefore, is that it is neither world, nor mother or father, nor God, but *something else*. The first thing that happens to the child—to every person—is that it is spoken to. It is smiled at, entreated, rocked, comforted, punished, given presents, or nourished. *It is first a "you"* to a powerful being outside itself—above all to its parents. For this reason, Goethe was correct when he wrote in *Pandora*, "A father is always a god." He is so because he is present for his daughter *before her own "I"* is, and because he bestows upon her the consciousness of herself by addressing her as "you".[1]

Hearing others say that we exist and mean something to them, and that they want something from us, precedes our articulating that we ourselves exist and our articulating what we ourselves are. We develop self-consciousness by receiving commands and by being judged from outside. In the face of these commands and judgments, we perceive that we are someone special, and being something different or special is the fundamental experience of an "I". And how many people achieve nothing in the course of their lives besides this dull, defiant feeling of "otherness," a fact brought home by the sentence "I am I", the first sentence of all psychologies and ethics of the individual. "I am I" is the answer of a person who is addressed, by name, from outside, just as many children time and again speak of themselves by self-confidently using their own names.

A person's being addressed by his own distinguishing proper name precedes any thinking about himself that he may later do as an "I". Accordingly, the shortest principal part of a verb (in Semitic, as well as Indo-Germanic languages) is the "you" form of the imperative: go, come, listen, be, become. Only after hearing that does man respond—defiantly, self-confidently—"I am I", a man who is distinguished by a proper name, unlike the classifiable things of the outside world: trees, tables, stones, or houses. This makes it

---

1. In this book the German *du* is generally translated as "you"; it can also be translated and understood as "thou".

clear to him that he can answer yes or no, that he can resist. The well-known way many stubborn children constantly say "No," is merely a practical application of the fundamental experience of answering "I am I".

The things of the world which man names but which do not answer him and cannot address him, the third persons, the "it"s, are discovered only in a third step. It is significant that children and childlike people like to speak of themselves in the third person when they are not challenged and thus made stubborn and forced back into using "I". A child may talk about himself: "Hans rode the train. Hans is tired." A command, on the other hand, leads to and forces a "yes" or "no" answer. These two words are only apparently mere interjections. In actuality, they are expressions of the truly divine "I" personality, the foundations of the omnipotence given us. To say "yes" and "no" means to create and resist, to suffer and to create suffering. God says "yes" and "no," and we say it as sons of God.

But childlike people, in particular, don't always move through life using the omnipotent first person. As the hero in [Carl] Spitteler's *Imago* [1906] does with his "Konrad," they often relinquish their "I"s to the world of things, submerging themselves in it until a new command addressed to their "you"s startles and recalls them from the realm of the Adam within them. Then they tend to fall into the other extreme, the first person, because they consider the "I"s personality the only form for "personal" life.

The soul's grammar needs all three persons, all three of them. For the soul must allow itself to be addressed in divine moments as "I", in meditative moments as "it", but upon awakening and in falling asleep as "you". The soul wanders from "it" via the "you" to the "I" and vice versa. The soul often winces during these transformations, and being lazy, it tries to escape them. But the most essential insight for us is just this: *Every turning point in the life of the soul becomes apparent as an inflection of its grammatical person*, just as a change in its grammatical number does.

What we have said here of grammatical "persons" also holds for the so-called moods: the indicative, the subjunctive, the imperative. Just as the persons characterize the appearance of the soul in its different moments, so the moods represent its primary method of acting during these moments. Customary grammar records everything: I sing, you sing, he sings; that I might sing, that you might sing, that he might sing; sing, he ought to sing, we ought to sing, etc. And so it proceeds through every tense and every mood in the active and passive voices, in the singular and the plural, as if all parts could be interchanged at will. The beautiful tables in textbooks actually seem to suffer because they lack an imperative form in the first person singular. The soul's grammar, on the other hand, discloses primary and secondary relationships between persons and moods. It distinguishes primal statements from mere developments and derivations. The latter cause primal statements to enrich one another; they bring them closer together and intertwine them. But this fully developed mesh should only be understood as superficial filling between the deep primal eruptions or expressions of the soul's creative, shaping power.

Grammar taught in school uses lists of conjugations, which are photographs of the surface of the linguistic world, where the phenomena appear side by side. The streams of speech which originally erupt from within the soul are something different from the utilization to which they are put in the everyday lives of men. The standard philosophies of language deal only with the utilization of primal speech. Everyday life utilizes each of the soul's original achievements for its own ends. So it creates rational and informative language, and expedient language, which is used as a means, a tool. Businessmen, above all, treat speech as if it were something stored and readily available, like currency or small change. The more novel their commodities, the more stereotyped and polished their spiels to infuse trust in people.

But what kind of philosophy is this? It mistakes this exploitation, this minting of the soul's golden utterances, for the essence of language. This superficial philosophy posits an artificial network of expedient sewer technology as the essence of the fountainhead of speech which erupts so overpoweringly in men. It confuses the ability to speak with the necessity to speak. Everything a human being *has* to do, he and those like him *can* do. The ordinary person in us *can* do only what others have *had* to do. When a person is confronted by the need to speak, however, he no longer sees speech as a tool by which he can make himself understood. Rather, he is seized by speech because things demand to be understood by him; because a man wants to be fully comprehensible or because God wishes to become audible to him. Notice the difference: to make oneself fully comprehensible is the desire of the whole person in us, of the whole "man-man." The man-fox, the man-wolf, and the man-snake (which Cyprian already distinguished from the whole man-man), they, to be sure, wish only to make themselves intelligible.[2] They want only to order something from a waiter, something that is on the menu, to close a deal on a product, or to exchange a conventional courtesy. They want to pass on something ready-made. A man-man, by contrast, will find a song of love or hate, of weakness or strength, of fear or joy, since the original body of speech within him wants to make him fully comprehensible.

A song, however, is nothing other than the "I" form taking shape within the resonance of the subjunctive or the optative. The will is freeing itself here, which is reflected in the lovely name "volunteer" [German, *Freiwilliger*]. "Voluntative" would be the right name for these ways of speaking, if the thinkers had not added the squabble over the freedom of will. We all know about volunteers and their good will. We experience ourselves as volunteers! We know of the freedom of God as well. But we know nothing about an abstract freedom of our will. On the other hand, the animals, plants, and matter outside, as well as the wolf or fox within us, become pacified when we can understand them—or more precisely, when the human being within us can understand them. The form of language through which the world of things enters us is rational language, passed off nowadays as original language. When we "move about in the world," when we want to take action effectively as men of the world, we have to continue using the old concepts for things. For we do not speak *with the world* as we do with our

---

2. Presumably St. Cyprian, Bishop of Carthage, martyred 258.

equals. Within the world, the extraordinary feat that the "man-man" in us can perform gives things their *correct* names.

The old saying that the world would come to an end if one person in it were once to tell the full truth, is not an exaggeration. The world, as a world of things, of third persons, of convention, always does collapse when a person accepts it as if it were human. And a person who does accept it also exceeds his own grasp, as he himself is a master of primal speech only at times. He is also a part of the superficial world. He dares to make a piece of the world human. On the other hand, when he happens to be in a contemplative or theoretical mood, he will even speak of himself in the third person, as a piece of the world, just as "Konrad," Carl Spitteler's hero, does.

As we come to know primal grammar, we find a connection between the indicative and the third person. Things controlled by the indicative are calmly dismissed into the world. The indicative describes and tells about things that are resting, that have been, that are finished or at hand. Since or insofar as philosophy was wisdom of the world, its first and everlasting question had to be about being. Being and existence are indeed the epitome of the indicative in all its varieties, because it allows "some thing" to be said about the world.

The subjunctive (the optative, the voluntative), the power and force of the "I"—full of glory in being a law unto itself—flows against the restrictive discipline of this stream of thought. The subjunctive is a rising chorus, the marching song of "coming to be" and of all those who are coming to be: "O, that I had a thousand tongues"; "If I for once were God." From the most sacred seriousness to the joke, the resonant power of the "I" always brings forth the subjunctive.

Therefore, when philosophy wants to become the "I's" consciousness, it speaks of "will" and "coming to be," instead of "existence." The philosophy that deifies man is called Idealism, since it thrives on freedom of the will. Freedom, however, is the most pithy expression for the subjunctive, which expresses everything coming to be. Freedom is the most pithy expression for not wanting to obey yet the laws of existence, for wishing to think of oneself not as a part of the world but as divinely inspired, as an Idealist.

Love is without wish or will, forgets self, has no freedom for self. "And if I were to choose him, it would be no choice at all." Love forgets the world as well. "If I have but thee, if thou art mine, what do I care about heaven or earth?" For the stream of the spirit that gives birth to the language of love, what remains from a mating call to a responsible call of duty but the "you"? Love doesn't dally like a flirt, playing around with small talk. Love transforms. It implores and commands. So the "you" [or the "thou"] is virtually discovered for the first time in the imperative, which arises from the transformation love creates.

If there were a philosophy based on the "'you' to whom I am closest," in addition to philosophies based on "views of the world" and philosophies based on self-consciousness, then philosophers would long ago have found their way out of the indicatives of laws of the world and subjunctives of free will to a complete grammar. But there is no such philosophy and there cannot be one. For philosophers, in fact, have been either self-forgetting or forgetful of the world, but never both—*never mere Samaritans of thought.* When that happens to them, they stop philosophizing. Herman Cohen, the last of the great German Idealistic philosophers, owes the greatness of his last work to this: It speaks from the "you" of faith. It stops being philosophy!

However, we may move a step closer to the grammar taught in schools. Each verb tense also has a special affinity with a specific mood. The indicative, for instance, is originally not in the present tense. It recounts things that have come to be, that have been, or things that have passed or are passing in the universe outside the speaker. In Greek, derivations of the aorist tense (past indefinite) represent the pure indicative. To express the present indicative, on the other hand, the aorist form is often merely lengthened or re-duplicated!

All subjunctives are in the future tense by their very "nature." It is only the imperative that captures the pure present, the point where the past turns into the future, where what is coming is pulled into the here and now. The imperative is the mood of transformation, the mood of the powerful exclamation, "*Tolle, lege,*" "*Tolle, lege,*" "take and read," that once brought Augustine to his real calling.

This last point especially seems a surprising discovery in view of the prevailing maltreatment of the soul's grammar. For now at last we can comprehend fully what the wisdom of the world and Idealist theories of freedom have done to the poor psyche. To the occultist, it is something material; to the philosopher, it is free. Both cheat the psyche out of its love-filled present. It can never fully enter the present while under their control.

The occultists—and all materialists—praise the psyche's substantial quality of being, that is, the part of it that conforms to rules, its being bound up with existence, its existence. They praise that for being its true form. Philosophers, however, preach that its true task is dreaming of freedom, reason, and immortality. So both create a virtual reality made out of rules or tasks, a reality that is meant to replace the real, demanding present, ruled by love as it is. That impoverishes the lyre of the soul. They want one string as a surrogate to sound tones that should come from other strings.

The soul can choose between all the moods and tenses, just as it can among the three grammatical persons. The soul can reverberate with the melody of things to be, as well as resound in the chord of present existence or in the rhythm of transformation. It can repose in the grave of the past, soar into the heaven of promise, or serve its days on earth. But the one-sided and single-stringed theories of grammatical thinkers such as "I"-oriented philosophers or matter-oriented occultists have a downright soul-destroying effect. They discourage the soul from putting up all the strings placed at its disposal by the grammar of its speech.

The soul's grammar, however, is strong enough to do more than just ward off the soul-destroying effect of specialized knowledge (philosophy in all its varieties) and secret knowledge (occultism). It treads a fine line between them both. But beyond that, it puts the whole colorful catalogue of spiritual and linguistic superficiality to a fundamental inner test—the catalogue peddled these days by the grammar taught in schools, by philology, literature, art history, the history of civilization, sociology, etc. Up to now, we have had only the superficial grammar, rhetoric, points of view, etc., that you get in schools, all derived from the *"artes liberales,"* the liberal arts of medieval elementary instruction.

These disciplines have often concerned themselves with the outside of words and sentence structures, dismissing as superfluous any insight into the basic laws of speech inspired by the soul. They continually confuse the life of the original fountainhead of speech itself with things derived from the original sources, mere technical extensions. They regard guiding children onto the track of adult speech (itself a sort of thorny hedge around a sleeping beauty) as an example of using primal, original language. But no one can tell whether the child, surrounded by this age-old thicket, will find the courage at any time in the course of its life to speak the redeeming Word, to speak its own original words from the depths of its soul.

Most people—children, too!—live superficially. Just as most could not have invented the wheel, neither could they have invented language! Most people can only utilize, imitate, and develop language or squash it flat. At best, we humans can speak primal language only at times and only temporarily. That is what Goethe meant in his important remark to Rieder on March 26, 1814: "People are only productive as long as they are also religious; otherwise, they become merely imitative and repetitious." [*"Die Menschen sind nur solange produktiv, als sie auch religiös sind; dann werden sie bloss nachahmend und widerholend."*]. A person is human already if he has experienced this power even once, and bowed respectfully to its divine splendor and omnipresent originality. For most, this occurs through the original words we use when we have to declare love. We should not be misled by the fact that this happens rarely. Rare as it is, this eternal originality keeps speech alive.

In their speech, souls have always had to renew and reproduce the truth of primal grammar. They still do today. Otherwise, the primal grammatical persons, the primal moods, and the primal tenses would have become extinct long ago. Original outbursts are kept alive by re-erupting within people. Once articulated, the primal sentences of inspired mankind take shape, and time and again need to be re-awakened with a kiss, by being transformed in the eyes and hearts of each newly "called" generation. As Goethe said: "*(Auf, in der holden Stunde stosst an und)* küsset treu bei jedem neuen *Bunde die alten wieder neu*!" "Awaken in the blessed hour and faithfully with every new union kiss alive the old ones anew."

This is more than just a song, it is a profound truth. The older *strata* of history stay alive only as long as ongoing *events* are touched anew by God's calls. Every spiritual stage of a people—for example, the history of Athenian literature, or the cultural history of the Occident—*represents a process of keeping alive the stream of speech that once gave birth to simple sentence structures, by constantly re-transforming it.*

An example may make this clear: epics, poetry, and drama are primal grammar exponentially unfolded. The realm of the outside world is as clear in epics as the realm of the exuberant, enthusiastic first person is in poetry. In drama, we can even recognize the "you". As both the third-person chorus and the full "I" of the *deus ex machina* start letting the hero have his say, he starts becoming fully human. He responds to the command of the deities by awakening to a defiant, god-like, nay-saying self-awareness. Answering the message of the gods from his stage between God and world, between poetry and epic, Prometheus defies the orders of the Olympians and begins to speak the pure, present-tense language of the human soul. Springing from defiance, that language will die away, fulfilling ancient drama, die away in the drama of the cross, die away in obedience. That initial defiance is an attempt by self awareness to be god-like instead of being a "you", and it is being defiant only because it is weak. That weakness, the defiance of man when he is summoned, constitutes tragedy.

The forms of ancient literature (as they were originally understood) correspond to elements of primal grammar. With that in mind, European art, science, and legislation can also be seen as the carefully tuned strings of a musical instrument—a people—upon which the spirit is playing. Science contains the world of space, the world that is described in the third person and the past tense. The fine arts carry us off into the heavenly light of genius, i.e., into the life of the first person. But only commands and laws, telling people what they have to do, anchor the arts and sciences in time at a certain hour. The law of the *polis* (the Greek city), for example, was ranked higher than the Greek arts and sciences.

This ability to live in the second person, however, will disappear from a people that loses itself entirely in its self-consciousness or in the world of space. Indeed, in the course of the last centuries of scientific experimentation and the formation of powerful nation-states, we can see that the legislative language of "thou shalt" has been withdrawing more and more from the European people into a few hands and heads (sovereigns or parliaments). The knot of the imperative—our real guarantee of a healthy life in the second person—is being loosened.

The separation between the "outer" life of government and law and "inner" conviction and morality—this is the infamous theory of German inwardness. This separation of state authority and personal morality only means that a people has renounced living in the second person, living a fully human life, as it is generally understood. The development of the modern state is making people into statistics, into *objects* of legislation, into third person individuals. Using the bureaucratic apparatus, sovereigns were experimenting with the people as if they were pieces of nature. The state is turning into a god, into a subject, into a reason become flesh that speaks in the first person, and so is godlike. So between the state's being a first person, and its treating people as third persons, all that is left for the soul is the categorical imperative of legally pre-established duty. The only thing it isn't meant to be is a loving, listening, obedient soul, a soul with the power to transform itself, a soul which fuses law and ethics by suffering, a soul which asserts itself by acting, a soul beloved of God.

Obviously, the final result and offshoot of this impoverished life are those activists who march forth victoriously whenever it suits their sovereign egos, but who always do so at the wrong time, and unbidden. The species of military politicians, goal-oriented activists, and flat-chested female communists belong to that brand. They don't know what it's like for a soul to be at peace.

At the least, people who are merely active, this class of military and civilian intellectuals like [Erich] Ludendorff [d. 1937] or Kurt Hiller [d. 1972]—and they are cut from the same cloth![3]— have no inkling that individuals, groups, and peoples are perfectly matched in one respect: they can remain at peace with themselves only by changing and being transformed. An activist, ever resolute, may not be macho personally, and may have peace within his own soul, but he imagines that a people in its entirety follows a different path to peace than an individual does. Primal grammar proves the universal validity of transformation.

For a human soul must have lived through a lot before it can assume the first-person form, "I". Even the power of the "I", though god-like in its purposefulness, remains only one of the primal elements along with the two others. A person who isn't always capable of living also in the third and second persons, is not a god or a hero, but is his ego's fool. Such a group of men is a band of warriors, a torch, or an army, but not a people. For a people are called "a people" because of their power to change; because they never freeze in the stance of the first person.

An "I" does not single itself out on its own, but is singled out by voices from the outside. This singling out is the process of life itself. A soul is summoned by an appeal to its proper name. The relationship between that summons and the soul's answer as an "I", will remain the same throughout all the stages and levels of its life. All self-recognition, all of an "I"'s self-knowledge, is produced by summons, by an individual's definite feeling that a concrete challenge has hit home. His childhood gods wane, as do those of his father and mother, or of anyone else. The entire wealth of spiritual heritage may assume their place: model heroes, clouds of witnesses, figures of the poets. The imperative may erupt from unexpected sources, but it is always the imperative that forces a soul to come forward and that unfolds its powers into the realm of the body as well as that of the spirit.

3. Ludendorff was a general, Hiller a pacifist.

The sequence of "you" to "I" is part of the constitution of the soul and is preserved through all stages of life, the ages of adolescence or young adulthood notwithstanding. To be sure, a person in his twenties often abandons the gods of his youth when he abandons the views of his parents. The child's heaven is being dismantled. But the apparent rulers of the child's soul—parents, teachers, dear God with his white beard—are not replaced by a vacuum. On the contrary, a person now learns to pay even more attention to voices that do not come from visible mouths. He begins to hear the voices of politics (i.e., of the times), of the people, of faith, of philosophy, of love, as invisible voices within him. By making demands, they begin to urge him toward a new self-chosen position in life, toward his vocation. These invisible voices determine a person's destiny—an "I"'s destiny—and woe to him if he cannot distinguish the voice of God from the voice of the tempter during this time of change.

To be sure, the god-like power of the "I" is erupting here. And youths nearly break apart under their sense of mission, their need to strive for the infinite. But a youth doesn't become a man until the hour when, for the first time, he lets the last stage of his growth, his first person, be transformed again, when he again obeys and suffers. He hasn't lived as a whole person until this moment, as someone comprised not only of "I", but also of "you" and of "it", who varies and changes between these forms. Our study of the soul should lead us to introduce the grammatical sentence, "God has called me, therefore I am," to replace Descartes' "Cogito, ergo sum" (I think, therefore I am), which is merely pure logic, like "I am I" or "A equals A." I have been given my own name, therefore I am. The simple declaration of my "being here" is the most profound and purest response I can offer to someone addressing me by name. It only takes a part of me to contradict a specific order or to stand up to a particular challenge from the outside. But there is neither petty detail nor mere coincidence in the answer: "You have called me, and I am here." It encompasses all conceivable answers. So this has always been considered the greatest answer. It is as free of mere abstract thinking as of mere defiance. The Adam within us, being either defiant or afraid, has avoided giving this answer since the first day of creation (as everyone knows).

Abstracting, however, is only a convenient learned expression for the process of withdrawing oneself, of taking flight. A clever man just recently re-diagnosed philosophy as dread of the world and fear of death. In point of fact, all "abstracting" is an attempt to escape a here-and-now concrete situation by weaseling out of the responsibility of answering, "I am here, and this is what I am."

Matthias Claudius turns the above maxim around somewhat.[4] But his emphasis raises "I am" very nicely to a principle of awareness gained by a responsive soul once it dares to live in the second person:

> I thank God and am happy
> Like a child with Christmas presents
> That *I am, am*! (And that I have you,
> Beautiful human countenance!)

> *Ich danke Gott und freue mich*
> *Wie's Kind zur Weihnachtsgabe,*
> *Dass ich bin, bin! (Und dass ich Dich*
> *Schön menschlich Antlitz! habe).*

Only by being thankful and thinking of God does joy in one's own personal existence swell into that unsurpassable doubling of "I am."

So we see, the soul should be man's answer to God, although it can be misused to answer whatever gods and idols it chooses to. However, even the crudest idolizing of an "ism" keeps the soul more vital than it is when it's merely deaf. Any kind of life in the second person is better than none. "Man should obey, woman should serve." (Goethe). Living creatures become animated when they are answering "you"s, "you"s that answer the living God.

Only dead or dying people have become the sort of finished "I" that modern scientists deal with, following ancient patterns. In the eyes of psychologists who base their thinking on the "I",

---

4. Matthias Claudius (1740–1815) was a German poet.

therefore, the soul is a dead soul, a deceased soul. The corruptness of our nature has allowed psychological experiments and research to produce a few alleged achievements, despite the fact that psychologists posit a soul that is dead, that is a thing, or that is at best an athlete of reason. Of course a lot of us have successfully avoided having inspired souls, meaning that the power of our souls has either never been awakened, or has died young. We all have a bit of dead "it" and dead "I" inside us. And psychological experiments are designed around this residue of the soul. They base their approach on our malformations, our sins, and on the brutish and dead bits of us. Luckily, man is not so entirely God-forsaken that he cannot, time after time, become a child of God again by becoming a "you". Psychologists labor like Sisyphus over a corpse of a soul.

In concluding this first sketch of the soul's grammar, we can now say what grammar is: the discipline of changing from one form into another. Its contents are variation, transformation, and changes of time. German grammar, as taught in school, recognizes umlauts and ablauts; primal grammar recognizes changing from one form into another!

As part of a universal—or better yet, fundamental—primal discipline of changing from one form into another, we can admire again the grammar taught in schools. In fact, it is an enormous achievement for men to be able to use all the grammatical persons —"I love, you love, he loves"—and for *each and every man*, in the course of the ages, to have appropriated these changes of person, tense, and mood. It is just as just as astonishing and misleading as the fact that each and every man can pray, command and obey, tell a story, sing, and that nowadays everyone learns to think, calculate, and write poetry.

The most primitive grammar already contains the entire miracle of being human as fully as does the most advanced "culture." People have received the former as well as the latter from a few original creators, and frequently their ability to manipulate either is only an illusion.

6

The Fate of the Soul

WE HAVE GONE TO sufficient lengths to make the point that both occultism and psychology commit the same error the Greeks did. They assume that an "I" or "it" precedes a "you", while in reality both are *answers to the "you"*, or longings for the "you". They can offer meaningful insights only as responses to our longings for a command from someone who loves us.

This Greek attitude has the most devastating effects in prophecy and magic where the answer as an answer is still retained clearly. A person certainly must receive a calling to become a prophet or a miracle-worker, otherwise he may not prophesy or try to heal. Prophesying and miracle-working may only be done at the right moment, in their own time. It is sacrilege to try either without a calling. The Greek mentality, or to use a better expression, the pagan mentality, does not recognize that the entire realm of our existence as souls is beyond our arbitrary control, that it has to give an unintentional answer to the question and to the calling of our particular lives.

Lack of this insight has been most devastating where the greatest effects are ascribed to individuals. The occultists, for example, turn prophecy into fortune-telling, and miracle-working into sorcery. They let demonic beings have their way, their rigid way, instead of leaving it to souls who have a calling for it. A Catholic clergyman, Staudinger, wrote a book on experimental magic, its demons and manifestations.[1] The book shows that a man's belief in a religious creed has little influence on errors of the spirit like these. The occultists' method coerces people into believing in it, and swallows up anybody who employs it. Scientific psychology is rooted in the same fundamental error.

Scientists also believe that isolating "I" is a free act by this "I", or a "fact" about it. Belief in this obscures the real difference between *selecting* the status of an "I", which is the necessary result of the whole process of life, and the *sin* of intentionally being an egomaniac. So they deny the borderline between health and sickness. For a relatively unimportant reason, this mistake has a less devastating effect on science than on occultism. Scientists put the "I" aside, under glass, avoiding the danger posed by its Satanisms and their permeation of the world. This works only because the scientists don't dare implement their error. They stop at the isolated "I". And by artificially isolating lots of abstract, formless "I"s, they rob the "I" of its worth in the world as a bearer of its own proper name.

But men demand their own proper names. For our proper names are what let us become carriers of our own souls and of our own particular fates. That's why men still run to occultists, for the time being. The occultists recognize at least that man is embedded in the world. To them, man is a cosmic being through whom the streams of nature are surging. On the other hand, they don't think he is a being that is spoken to. But a man who is not spoken to cannot become human. Without being summoned, he will remain what he was, a natural being, an animal. This is the line between white magic and black magic, between human and sub-human occultism.

The occult disciplines regard man as an animal, as a plant, as a piece of matter, as a conductor of power, as a reflection of the alignment of the sun and the planets, as a cosmic phenomenon. So they try to come to grips with him by calculating the paths of the

---

1. Possibly Josef Staudinger, d. 1958.

stars (astrology), by interpreting his body (physiognomy, graphology), by mesmerizing and hypnotizing him, by metamorphoses (transmigrations of the soul).

If an appeal to its living proper name doesn't single it out from the species, an individual "I" will remain a piece of earth, a piece, or a specimen, of the human world, or a piece of matter. This animal side of him becomes terrifying when he sets himself up as the arbitrary administrator of the natural forces that are whirling through him, when he practices magic, conjures up ghosts, or hypnotizes, just because he can do it, likes doing it, or wants to do it—or because somebody else wants it or likes it—rather than because he has to do it or ought to do it. He becomes terrifying when he practices his craft instead of acting in response to the voice of his conscience (that is, literally acting responsibly) and when he wants to conceal (occultus!) his power and so hide from being summoned by his name.

Thus, it simply isn't true that the occult disciplines are aimed at the "subconscious," or the "beyond," or some further, unnamable side of the soul. To avoid being contaminated by them, psychologists have taken cover behind claims like these, without justification. The occult disciplines do address the psyche, in its capacity as the bearer of a special fate. The field of scientific psychology, on the other contrary, addresses the concept of a "normal person's" soul, that of one individual among many, in studying the soul's physical and mental functions.

This is where the gaping contrast lies, and it can be made fruitful. The superstitions—astrology, spiritualism, palm-reading, theosophy—hinge on particular, single psyches. One psyche, and it alone, will suffer misfortune, be subject to transmigration of the soul, or act under the influence of Mars and Jupiter. So the occultist disciplines are second-hand disciplines which plunge into an area that the field of psychology carefully avoids: that of the unique fate of the unique individual soul.

Psychologists are right to reject the methods of these secret disciplines. But their own are not any better. Psychologists don't even bother to figure out that each person has a soul of his own—or *whether* he does—or what that might mean. If they had, they would have admitted that an insight they now flagrantly ignore is an axiom: Given two souls, two groups, two peoples, the same external behavior, the same "reaction" will never mean the same thing in terms of the souls concerned. When two people are doing the same thing is precisely when it cannot turn out to be the same thing. The reverse follows from this (and is very significant for the life of peoples): When two people are doing something different, it may well turn out to be the same thing!

The field of psychology will continue to be overtaken by pseudo-sciences and superstition (which is what's happening today) as long as it lacks the courage to raise the question about the fate of the individual human soul. It behaves as if this aspect of the soul had not existed certainly and unmistakably for ages. Every verse, every picture, every proverb, every singing eighteen-year-old girl attests to this. Psychologists refuse to admit it. The idealistic psychologists may be right in refusing to subordinate the soul to natural concepts of rigid experimental regularity. But all the same, isn't the soul rooted in the womb of the created world, until it receives its calling?

On the other hand, the empirical psychologists may be right in refusing to acknowledge that the soul has the freedom of a boundless creature of the spirit. But does that mean the soul has no history of progress toward its salvation? The field of psychology may have to refuse to explain the properties of the soul on the basis of the physical appearance of the body, but does that mean the soul has no ability to express itself in the body?

The microcosm of the soul is a parable of creation.
The essence of the soul fulfills itself as a life story.
The language of the soul transforms the world.

These three themes—phrased as questions or propositions—contain in any case the scientific problems posed by the soul, in the ecumenical sense of the word. No one is working on them today because psychologists presume that to deal with these issues they would have to act unscientifically. But for people in general, the whole field of psychology will not be a field of study of the soul if it does not give them an answer to precisely these three questions, namely:

How can the superstition of a transmigration through jackal, swine, or lotus-flower be replaced by a doctrine of a history of a path through life that fulfills the soul?

How can the superstition that people are chained by numerical combinations to matter or to the world of stars be replaced by a doctrine in which the insignificant, individual man—or even the great man, mankind—is transfigured into an embodiment of all cosmic powers, into a microcosmos?

How can the superstitions arising from the laws of palmistry, phrenology, and handwriting analysis be replaced by a doctrine that explores the power of the soul to create, explores its bearing and its revelation, those powers that blast open the prison walls between individuals?

7

The Powers of the Soul

THESE ARE NOT EXAGGERATED or religious or unscientific questions. They have very immediate practical consequences—also as far as psychology is concerned. For instance, if the soul has a history, then it will have to be constituted by forces quite different from those governing the psychologists' "psyche." They would be those forces that carry it through time, providing a bridge through time from birth to death. So *courage* and *fear* would become the sustaining factors for a psychology of the individual soul; typically up to now, they have been relegated to the sphere of morals! Courage and fear, however, have nothing to do with conventional ethics.

To make any sense of souls generally, all of a soul's individual, momentary expressions (perception, association, thought, etc.) have to be based on these continuing lines of force, these bridges through time. It is exceptional and rare to perceive things when one is indifferent. A living person perceives out of fear, out of hope—or at least in fear and hope. So the more soul he has, the more completely he will fail psychological experiments, because they collect things and stock them. But the soul faces its historical realization every moment, faces the either-or of dangerous decisions. Further, if fear and hope are the shaping powers of the inner sphere of the soul, then crises and catastrophes in the life of the soul deserve scientific attention, an additional circumstance that, to date, the field of psychology has anxiously avoided. In every field of study, the decisive step from scholasticism to science starts at the point at which the exceptions, the crises, become explainable. In linguistics, the laws of phonetics have done it; in economics, the theories of crises; in jurisprudence, the study of revolutions; in history, the study of cessation of history, of the decline and fall of peoples. Traditional jurisprudence reveals that it is scholasticism because it has—or to the degree that it has—anxiously avoided the problem of revolutions.

Psychology does not even recognize the problem of crises of the soul! That is why an abyss separates it from psychiatry. As soon as we recognize that fear and hope encompass the realm of the soul, we can finally see that catastrophe is the central event in its life. In a catastrophe, the soul maintains its identity, is one and the same, despite a physical accident, spiritual re-evaluation, reversal, or reorganization. The soul's web of life spans obstacles that are neither materially "natural" nor "logically" clear. Through this paradox the soul proves that it can pierce the shell of the world, that it is not some product of thought, but that it was really born into the world, that it is not yet dead, that it has not yet let its powers turn to dust, but rather that it uses them as it travels through life.

The soul tries to assert itself, resisting both mind and body. Whether a nervous breakdown or a complete catastrophe, a crisis provides its best chance of confirmation. A person who avoids a crisis evades the soul-shaping task set before him. Crisis, the external process which breaks in upon the soul, corresponds to the power to endure it, the soul's ability to bear pain. The ability to suffer is the achievement of the soul, which anchors, so to speak, the bridges through time, fear and courage, in the abyss of the period over which they are to carry us. Each pain is a pier that ties the course of the soul firmly to reality and roots it to the ground. The deeper the suffering the soul "goes through"—as language puts it so poignantly—the more forcefully it enters reality, the more significant the event is for the soul's history, since it has to overcome ever more worldly facts that are external to the soul itself.

This "overcoming," "undergoing," or even "striving," as poets like to call it, occurs completely in the solitude of the individual soul. It is fighting a battle against the outside world. The fruit of this lonely battle is the shape of the soul. For when a striving to take shape carries the soul over an abyss of material obstacles and logical contradictions, the whole course of a person's life from birth to death becomes a unity. This unity is not built up out of individual stages of the person's life, but rather, the unity itself invests the stages with sense and meaning. What we have said about every single momentary action is also true of the ages of human life. They are not just states the soul is in, since the soul is also always *resisting* the spirit of any particular stage of life, and resisting the condition of one's body at any particular time of life. Each stage of life threatens us—that is, threatens our soul—-just as much as it molds us. A practical study of the soul has to deal with the tasks the soul faces in the individual stages of life. That stops life from being a mere aging process. The soul needs to use the resources of each stage of life in striving for a fulfillment appropriate to it.

To an outside observer, the process inside a soul remains as indistinct as the psyche of a patient is to his doctor (about which we spoke above). Teachers, ministers, and lawyers are in no better position than the physicians, for the simple reason that nothing is impossible for God, and that everything is possible for the soul. An outside observer only knows after the fact how the soul has fought and won. But our basic principles are of tremendous help. The earlier stages of a life gain their full meaning from its consummation, and not until then. Only death gives the preceding life its final meaning. Until death, the pattern of every soul is open to change. An observer will derive the standards he needs to fit a life together from its death and from all deathlike events within it (sickness, collapse, decay, etc.). Neither one's predispositions, nor one's nature, nor one's inherited talents disclose one's soul. Rather, a person's biography unrolls life from the time of death, starting with the final casting of a consummated human life. Instead of always looking at lives from birth forward, as it now does, the whole field of psychology should look backward. By keeping death in mind, it should learn to see even unconsummated lives correctly. Death provides the knot that finally connects all the separate events of a life. Until then, the significance of any event is still interchangeable with that of any other. The life of the soul awakens only in a person who boldly affirms the law of death and crises. Concepts and abstractions yield a cowardly view of life. Events and facing them head on yield a courageous view. A crisis, after all, is a forestalled piece of death. The crises in a life are its stations that give it its meaning. A life like that rises above trite divisions into luck and misfortune. Being risky anyway, such a life won't pass unblessed as long as it remains above luck or misfortune and true to the pure character of risk. "Blissful is the person who has passed the test"—that does not mean: How pleasant it is to rest on one's laurels. It means instead: Blessed is the person who—despite the temptations of pleasure and pain—resolutely subordinates himself to his soul, who does not disintegrate into body and spirit, into "material interests" and "spiritual hobbies," in the face of the dread that befalls every soul. Blessed is the person who entrusts all the fragments of his or her life to that formative power, to the risk of being shaped into what you and only you are called upon to become and are allowed to become.

That bit of natural life brought into the world as a child, entrusts itself, curiously enough, only to a soul that acts as a *thou*, as a soul addressed by God and called upon by God. Whenever souls become addicted to themselves, addicted to the intellect, or crave the glitter of the world, body and life immediately escape their control. This destroys a person's whole being by splitting it dreadfully into soul-fragments, into isolated bodily functions, into reluctant thoughts. If this whole being is predisposed to being filled with soul, it will remain intact only if it is progressively permeated with more and more soul.

How many diseases have their origin here! And in their stead, how many pseudo-diseases stemming from pseudo-causes are being treated in hospitals and sanatoriums? The world of doctors, lawyers, and politicians seems to be conspiring to help individuals hide from the fact that they are suffering from disintegration of their souls. And with their worldly wisdom, philosophical psychologists are even worse. Their abstractions continually goad us into becoming one-sidedly subjective or objective, so that a soul finds it hard to remain faithful to the knowledge that it must transform itself.

8

Community

BUT STUDY OF THE soul also leads beyond the individual soul. If courage and fear establish the limits of the soul, it becomes clear what "people being able to rely on one another" means in terms of the soul. In the act of trusting, the soul feels that it is relieved of a part of its task in life, the part that another soul has taken over from it. Channels of relief and connection are opened from soul to soul, by means available only to souls. These processes of relief counterbalance the soul's ability to suffer and to endure crises. It would not be able to bear the burden without some possibility of a counterbalance. While the soul is utterly alone in its battle with the world, in this instance, by contrast, parts of the outer world form a bond with it by becoming filled with soul. A sphere of the soul shared by several people emerges and enlarges (at the expense of the sphere of the body as well as that of the mind), and with that the stronger the inspiration and joint responsibility of the souls become. Souls joining together relieve the excess pressure of the world. A single soul would collapse the moment it fell prey to the chaos of the world, alone and far from its familiar highways and byways. Not so if it is buoyed by the confidence of other souls uniting with it in fear and hope, as well as in the ability to suffer in the face of death or unto death.

That is why we hear a cry for community today, with souls overburdened by danger and responsibility, as the traditional carriers of responsibility are stripped away. Unfortunately, that call is often voiced by materially-oriented or intellectualized people. They do not understand how vile they are, to externalize the soul's medicine of last resort, by making it an arbitrarily produceable and organizable slogan, a newspaper article, or the like. Meanwhile, this medicine, like any antitoxin, will retain its healing power only as long as it contains within itself the same life-threatening tension as the crisis it is meant to alleviate. Community is not a natural fact like the passion of an individual soul, but rather a way out, which cannot be sought without danger. Being a "way out," a union of souls necessarily dissolves the framework that protectively envelops a passionate soul.

Having laid out the central problems of the soul avoided by the field of psychology, we still have to say something about the framework. Psychologists know nothing about that, either. Here too, substitute sciences have appeared to occupy the terrain. When the soul searches out a path for itself through the changes of the body, or through the illusions of mental prejudices, it needs elbow-room, a husk, "space around its feeling," so that it can wax and wane, be affirmed and denied, be checked and praised. In the tension between fear and hope, the soul can shape itself only if it has a measure of freedom to experiment, a measure of uncommitted elasticity, when it is not subject at every moment to the public law of cause and effect.

Shame provides that elbow-room. Without shame, before shame, or beyond shame the soul does not grow. Shame is the housing that shelters anything connected with the soul. Shame is the grove in which anything to do with the soul has to be planted in order to grow. To an empiricist inquiring about it from naked, indigenous people, the shyness accompanying shame seems as arbitrary as it does to an idealistic psychologist, who considers it highly unreasonable. Shame does not fit the "system." If the soul were an "it" or an "I", i.e., an object or subject, a thing or God, it would certainly have no need of shame. Things and gods do not blush (see Homer!), nor do they tremble or sweat (remember Nietzsche's angry outburst, "A god who sweats!"). But a human soul, like you, conceals itself and shies away from things. This *verecundia* (shyness) is the way we appear primarily when living in the second person singular. The field of psychology can be judged lacking, both because it doesn't begin at shame and because it doesn't start with people's names. Both are ungrammatical attitudes.

The modern tendency toward a psychology of shame seems to represent a reversal of the trend, as does holistic psychology. But these trends still deal separately with two consequences of the same primal event, an event reflected to us by grammar and framed by the experience of shame. Vileness will destroy this framework. But a community of souls will grow only where the souls remain living souls, although they have overcome their shame. Bringing souls into communion doesn't require abolishing shame, but rather continually re-implanting the shame's field of force into one of higher tension.

The theory of diseases of shame, psychoanalysis, has not become clearly aware of this difference. Sometimes it aims to destroy shame, sometimes to overcome shame. That is why psychoanalysis has such a contradictory and ambiguous character. The soul cannot be healed simply by opening itself up and thus letting go of its own peculiar tension. The soul needs a cloak, something to clothe it against the world. Thomas Carlyle didn't smuggle the life of the soul arbitrarily into the "clothing philosophy" of his "re-sewn tailor" (*Sartor Resartus*). People have to walk about clothed; they have to be allowed to wear masks to protect them from the dead world. In everyday life one is masked. We are allowed to loosen this mask only when a higher power induces us to, when another human face looks at our own. Souls may only open themselves to other souls. The soul has to remain dead to the searching eye of the mind, or it will fall victim to it, which is what happens in psychoanalysis. A person may use the powers of the mind to explain a soul only if he is willing to pay for it with his own soul. That is why psychoanalysts (who are also "natural ministers of the soul") often-accomplish amazing things. They offer their own shame, their own souls, when encountering the souls of others; they gaze out of their own souls as much as they gaze into the souls of others.

9

The Speech of the Community

A "BORN" MINISTER OF the soul is also aware of the *arcanum*, of the secret remedy that will bind another, an unknown soul, to him. It is the mutual silence that falls before or after a word has passed between them. The language is being changed at that moment! From then on, both speak a different language, a new dialect. So there are as many dialects of primal language as there are changes of language that interrupt the world. There are as many dialects of primal language as outpourings of new streams of speech, which in mutual silence have overcome shame, and put to shame the awful claim that there are no bridges connecting man to man.

Because it is genuine, every such dialect bears within itself the possibility of becoming a full-fledged language in the usual meaning of the word, i.e., to add gradually a fully articulated surface structure to the stuff of its origin. The act of overcoming shame, always original, is a language's real point of origin, yesterday, today, and tomorrow, all the prize-winning essays on the subject notwithstanding.

We have about 10,000 languages on earth. To date, the Bible has been translated into 517 languages.[1] A translation of the Bible is the patent of nobility for every language; through that translation

---

1. *ERH*: "That was 1916. Today (1963) it is said to be more than 1,100."

it first becomes a language of culture, a full-fledged language of the soul. This is so because the story the Bible tells is a universe of histories, of souls as well as peoples..

But countless dialects also have what is needed to become "languages." Every group that suddenly falls silent when a key word is spoken, experiencing a change of language that arises from shame, has pushed through to the source of the life of speech, and thus becomes a carrier of primal language. Admittedly, the languages of most groups are a means to an end. They arise because they can, not because they must. Which is why students' slang, barracks lingo, or the argot of thieves are not reservoirs of primal language. In contrast, the dialect of the smallest mountain valley village is a speech-cell in the fullest sense, because fathers and daughters, mothers and sons, grooms and brides give voice in it to their transformations.

Now we can also recognize what the plural (about which we didn't speak above) means in grammar. To do that, we will have to break through the shell of school grammar. It is not an accident that languages distinguish between dual and plural. This doesn't refer to the difference between two and three, but rather to the different states of the soul which they express.

Modern superficial language, on the other hand, sees only something calculable in the plural: one plus one plus one. But "we" is not a plural in the sense that 10 chairs or 10 apples are. It was not 10 oxen that first shouted "*Te Deum laudamus*," but a "we" made up out of different first, second, and third persons: out of a father, a child, brothers and sisters, a bridegroom, a servant, a mother, a maid, a guest of honor, a beggar, a congregation, a household, a family. They all can find themselves in the hymn of praise of the three persons of the plural, we, you, and they. "Father, we praise thee, praise the Lord. The heavens are praising the glory of God." This means a "we" doesn't just cover up a bundle of identical uniform "I"s. That already is practical exploitation of the "we" by the marketplace. A "we" doesn't even cover the bonds between "you"s and "I"s who have found one another. That was the special function of the archaic "dual," nowadays submerged in the plural. In the genuine original plural, however—in the sense of a praying congregation, of all communities filled with faith, of any religiously alive original cell—in this original plural a piece of the world, that is, of some third person, has been fused together with pieces of "you"s and "I"s. Primal grammar fuses God, man, and world into a resounding *we*.

Whether the domesticated animals in the house of an animistic Sueven tribe participate in the life of the household and thereby join in the praise of God and the ancestors by flourishing astonishingly and so honoring the gods; or whether "the heavens are praising the glory of God, in all the lands resounds the word," the same law applies, in a single home as much as in the church of mankind. A piece of the world must loosen our tongues by *its* power to astonish. For amazement at the world awakens speech within the soul! And the second person steps up to join the third. Whether the father of the house asks the youngest child to say grace, or whether the congregation blesses the priest so that his spirit may become full of their spirit, an element of humanity in the second person—a "you" or "thou"—always has to enter the prayer.

Only being thus addressed keeps the priest or the child in the vibrating health of the unity of his soul. The child would be scared by the awesome task of facing God. But it is being called upon to do so. And when one obeys, one does not have to look to the right or to the left; one can forget about oneself. Without the command, "Now speak!", terror would split a soul in two. As is well known, the panic-like terror of the ancients has become fashionable again today among doctors as schizophrenia. We can understand now what that terror is. It is the mute and deaf terror, i.e., remaining speechless from terror that continues unrelieved by a liberating name or call. "The soul eludes consciousness at the high points of its life" (Holderlin). The soul is startled in the literal sense of starting or jumping aside. Being addressed in just the right way, however, turns this into the "sweet shock" of the angelic greeting. A person will stay healthy as long as someone talks to him, as long as he is addressed, whether in love or in hate.

The Speech of the Community

We hardly need to say that the third part needed to make up a community of "we" is the self-consciousness of an "I". "I"s suffer. Bodies that pray—be they bodies of people, households, or "I"s—start praying because they are sick, because they are suffering. An "I"s *suffering* loosens the tongue, just as the shock of a "Thou" and the amazement of an "it" do. And if more than just one, or another, or the third of these things befalls the soul, if all three come together, then all single forms of grammar are suspended. This is the language of prayer and worship. That is why the language of religion towers above the languages of science, art, and law-giving. It is the crown of languages because it leads the dance of the three grammatical persons, of the jubilance of "we"s, of the humility of "you"s, of the amazement of "they"s.

Religion in its daily life is just like art or science, a mere container of language. Primal words which erupted once, to be established and pronounced, are preserved in religion, as in other areas of life. "Religion" is only distinguished by the fact that its shrine preserves transformation itself, the secret of transformation.

The primal languages of the plural:

First Person (we)	*Second Person (you)*	*Third Person (they)*
Art	Legislation & (Transformation) Religion	Science

Having clarified the language of communities, we can complete the grammar we have started. The grammar outlined in Chapter Five has to subordinate itself to the one outlined here. Art represents the place of the first person plural—the person of transfiguration and apotheosis in the whole of our spiritual and intellectual life. But art contains as well the whole wealth of the three singular persons, in lyric, drama, and epic, for instance. This is no more of a contradiction than the fact that cells can recreate whole organisms. On the contrary, it shows that we have indeed made a discovery. We have come to an understanding of the uniform origin of the life of the soul and of the peoples.

The fields of learning can also be broken down into sciences of the world in the narrower sense of knowledge of space, of nature, and of numbers and measures; as well as into sciences of the "I": logic, philosophy, criticism; and into the teachings about the "you" and how it should conduct itself: jurisprudence, ethics, and history. Philosophy, in which the intellect lets everything revolve around the "I", starts with the assumption of eternal freedom. Natural science, emphatically revolving around the "it", starts with the principle of laws of nature. Jurisprudence, however (and ethics with its emphasis on "Thou shalt" or "I shall"), proceeds from legislation, from statutes, which are fought over, drafted, and issued, one way today but differently tomorrow! The body of legislation changes in its turn through the three grammatical forms of becoming, of being, and of application. The "I"s and the "we"s rule the political hurly-burly of legislation, of deliberations, of resolutions, of approvals and disapprovals, of the tally of votes, and the results of votes. They rule it with wishes, will, and liberties. The legal life of lawful citizens, of a pacified community, is ruled by unconscious habit and solidarity. Their holy order, like a second nature, makes the life of the nation a matter of blood, of instinct, and of descent. Freedom and peace thus surround the headwaters of the social and cultural life arising from the second person.

But when the order of this unconscious world is broken, the collapse frightens the soul of the people. The incidence of crime awakens its conscience, and to restore peace the responsible judge now consciously applies the statute that existed unconsciously until that moment. His sentence, "You are found guilty by the court," makes the person who broke the order of the world an outcast. It changes him into a solitary exiled soul. And if it wants to remain alive after being expelled, it will have to rebuild, and to reflect within itself from that time on, as an exile, the whole social order within which it had been allowed to live peacefully. The life of the nations is renewed and multiplied by exiles like that. That is the story of Jesus, for example.

That's enough to tie together the grammar of Chapter Five and the grammar presented here. As we have seen, however abundantly other grammatical persons have been made part of the languages of art, of law, or of knowledge, each language is governed by one grammatical person and each has to remain faithful to its particular nature. A court's judgment is always the origin of law and thus the site of its renewal. This means that all human, true legislation, as well as the ethics of all nations are rooted in the "you". From this central point one can *also* apprehend politics and peace under law—but one is only apprehending them additionally. Even in an epic poem, art still has to let its basic tone resonate, its tone of apotheosis, of freedom, elevating the song into a hymn of liberty. Only individual "I"s and their genius renew art.

Finally, even idealistic philosophy has to proceed from consciously perceived facts, that is, on the basis of some kind of third-person existence and inventory of the world. Science without facts and objects is like art without singers, or law without application and enforcement.

We can note the following interdependencies:

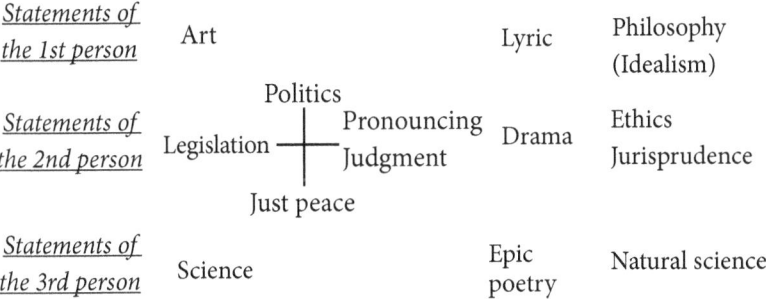

Pronouncing judgment is the "purest" order of society, but also the simplest. Lyric is the "purest" art but also the most rarified. Natural science is the "purest" science, but also the coarsest.

The fundamental principle of transformation, religion, has its own original statement of renewal in the secret of transubstantiation, but religion sends branches into the three other singular statements as well:

Sacrament ⎫
Mystery   ⎬ Fundamental principle: Transformation
Miracle   ⎭

1st person: Art *2nd person: Law* *3rd person: Science*
Liturgy   Theocracy   Theology
Cult   Church training   Dogmatics

Religion can't exist without miracles and transformation. No matter how artistically perfect the cult and liturgy may be, no matter how effectively the church may govern, no matter how the papacy, canon law, or theocracy may flourish, no matter how well theology may have fathomed all secrets and articulated them in powerful dogmas, the origin of religion lies in the fundamental principle of the "mystical marriage," the union of God and man and world, of "I" and "you" and "it".

A uniform order permeates the tree of language, ranging from the single leaf of a single sentence up into the crown of the highest spiritual and intellectual life. The superficial grammar with which the school system has been putting us off has to be plowed up, with the plow digging all the way down to the roots, right down to the matrices that guide things as they take shape, matrices whose influence reaches into everything spoken about, large or small.

The matrices of speech are found in stillness, in the silence that falls before words come into being. They are the preconditions, the conditions that *must be present* for us to think, write poetry, give orders, and pray. In order for primal speech to arise, people must first fall silent, into a silence rooted in the primal foundations of the soul, which manifest themselves by making people fall silent. Each primal foundation is represented by a different, primal form of silence.

The soul falls silent—we saw it in connection with shame—when another person startles it by addressing it. Being startled produces a silence within us, the silence of the second (grammatical) person at being addressed. The world causes us to fall silent in amazement; the wonders of the world are of the third person. The "I"'s god-like quality, however, causes it to fall silent when it suffers from itself. We fall silent while changing from one grammatical person to the other. We fall silent while changing from one person to another, when the transformation occurs between the suffering of the self-conscious and ingenious "I", and the fright felt by the "you" as it listens to inner voices and the amazement felt at the image of the physical world. We fall silent when we become aware of the unity of suffering, fright, and amazement and the unity opens up before us.

These are the primal conditions and preconditions of speech from which its single sentences, as well as its cultural creations, pour forth forever, renewing themselves daily. So it is appropriate also to liberate these primal sentences of the language from the masquerade forced on them by the terms used in schools. We should translate "indicative," "subjunctive (or voluntative)," and "imperative" on the strength of the primal words which rise from the roots of speech. Fortunately, we still have linguistic heritage rooted in this ground.

The translation of "indicative" is the easiest. The indicative states something about the world, it tells us what has happened, it answers the question: "What caused this miracle?" This question raises the question of causation. The world poses that question to us. Finding causes is the particular concern of worldly wisdom and natural science. The indicative produces causative or narrative statements.

The subjunctive has many names: optative, conjunctive, voluntative. In it, one's own will always establishes dependencies and moves people and things about eccentrically. The author is therefore the "I" of the artist, of the creative person. Something new arises from his spirit. Genius, spring-like, calls into the world of men, "Begin!" "When man falls silent in torment, God inspires him to tell of his suffering." "*Und wenn der Mensch in seiner Qual verstummt, gibt ihm ein Gott, zu sagen, was er leidet.*" (Goethe). The creative person, the giving person, the artist, answers the question, "What has been given to me, only to me, just to me, what are my 'talents,' what are the gifts I can make the most of?" And all this lets us summarize the subjunctive as the author's statement.

We can approach the author's statement from another angle by presenting it as an expression of freedom, of impending future, of fluid waves of the will. So it is a statement of will and choice, a can-do statement of eternal maybes, in contrast to the necessities of regulated cause and effect (the indicative).

The second grammatical person poses a more complicated problem. We shall be able to demonstrate the unfolding and partial decay of this primal form only in a future detailed study of language. Historically, this is where philosophy's substitute function in an ethical sense—that is, as more than worldly knowledge—has its origin. This is just as true for the language of law; it uses the imperative of the third grammatical person: *esto*.

It will suffice here to give the astonishing words "to be called" and "to command" their proper places as names of the imperative.[2] A commanding [*Geheiss*] statement both utters a name and gives a command. In one act, your "you" aspect is addressed, that which you represent to the caller, and you are shaped by your obedience. You are being "called" and now are "named" in accordance with what has happened to you.

These translations open up for us another area of language that we have not yet dealt with: the declension of nouns, the many cases in which nouns, "people, places, and things," can find themselves and through which they can move, from the nominative and the genitive via the dative and accusative to the vocative, the instrumental, and the locative. This essay is not the place to say the last word about our discoveries; in fact it is closer to being the first word. So it has to suffice to point out that the fourth case, the accusative, as well as the instrumental, belong with causative statements because they express causation. The second case (the genitive) is essential to commanding statements.

The genitive's, the patronym's, job is to indicate ownership and relationship. But the vocative, the call, is also part of this process, a process that leads from being called via being startled to

---

2. In German, "*Geheiss*," to command; "*heissen*," to be called or named.

being commanded. The nominative case arises from the author's statement, from the proud statement: "*Quos ego*." This well known statement expresses clearly an author's real striving to live up to the rules he sets for himself.[3] "How do I play by the rules? You make your own rule first, then follow it!" (*Meistersinger*). And these personal laws in turn arise in answer to a suffering person's question, "What can I do?" The "I" in men suffers from its freedom, from the thousand possibilities it can see before itself. It suffers from its doubts and from its right to choose. So it searches for its proper lot in life. "Here I sit creating men in my own image." "*Hier sitz ich, forme Menschen nach meinem Bilde.*" (Goethe's *Prometheus*).

The way verbs are conjugated nowadays no longer singles out the principal statement— which otherwise would have received its name from the silent revelation of the secret of transformation. Apparently, we have to call it the statement of origin.

>Indicative: Questions of the 3rd person: Wonder.
>Answer: Causative statements (causative cases).
>Imperative: Questions of the 2nd person: Fright.
>Answer: Command statement (command cases).
>Subjunctive: Questions of the 1st person: Suffering.
>Answer: Author's statements (author cases).
>————[4]: Questions of the fundamental statement: Secret.
>Answer: Statement of origination (revelation).

---

3. The "well-known" phrase is from the *Aeneid* (Book I, l. 135) and means literally "Whom I", indicating resentment at extreme impertinence by someone to whom much has been given. The context is a great storm at sea, destroying the Trojan fleet, which was apparently let loose by Juno, Neptune's vindictive sister. In the translation by C. Day Lewis, Virgil writes: "He [Neptune] summons the East and West winds, and then proceeds to say: / Does family pride tempt you to such impertinence? / Do you really dare, you Winds, without my divine assent / To confound earth and sky, and raise this riot of water? / You, *whom I* —! Well, you have made the storm, I must lay it."

4. *ERH*: Maybe the "participle" should be considered a special form of transformation, because it is essential to prayer. But this is advanced with all possible reservation

It is instructive to apply these prototypes to the real powers of history. Theologians, for instance, often prefer to retreat to authors' statements, to authority, rather than to originality, to revelation. Scientists would rather merely dictate than cause things. Artists try their hardest to be original in the sense of offering revelations of the secret of transformation instead of remaining creative in the sense of using existing things in a talented, original way, being able and artistic.

We have now translated grammar to the point where we can apply it politically. We had to get this far. Our new method should not remain mere tinkling words. It has to be fruitful, usable, and applicable vis-a-vis the powers of history and vis-a-vis communities of souls and peoples. We either belong to them or we do not; they exist or we miss them.

Primal statements are indispensable. They correspond to the fundamental inclinations of mankind. So they give us standards by which to evaluate communities. That standard is just what we have been missing up to now, which is why all the talk about politics and the people, about morality and individual souls, has been so sterile and ineffective. Here, however, we have a tool that can be scientifically tested.

At the outset, we can conclude that if communities are not rooted in any of these fundamental inclinations of the soul, they can only be considered superficial associations. The *intentions* of the people who "want," "create," "preach about" these associations don't change this at all. That these associations are non-binding is a phenomenon entirely beyond their control. People in these associations speak only a superficial language, good only for making themselves intelligible to one another, merely a derivative technique developed by someone else. Despite the best intentions, this way of speaking rings hollow and leaves the soul cold. One cannot use substitutes to bring the fundamental inclinations of the soul into play. In this world, people merely try to make themselves intelligible. Comparing research in this realm of intelligibility with the primal origins of things shows that the research is not so much a disciplined investigation of causes as it is a passionate obscuring

The Speech of the Community

of them—thus, errors; not so much the establishment of guiding rules as passing the buck—thus injustice; not so much vigorous authorship as a feeble usurpation of power—thus lies; not so much a loving spontaneity as hateful obduracy—thus, sin.

The lies and errors of human associations are not reproaches against their individual members, but statements about superficiality in general. A society as a whole isn't mendacious because people in society are liars. Rather, people "in society" have to lie because society is interested in power, not strength. The mass of people is not ignorant because the individuals in it are wrong. The individuals have to make mistakes because people in a mass are interested less in disciplined investigation of causes than in passionate obscuring of them. Individual states aren't unjust because their followers or judges want to be unjust. Their laws and courts are unjust because the single state can undertake only the shifting of guilt. Of course, in addition, love or suffering may corrupt the individual judge, making him even more unjust than necessary.

The individual believer may be even more obdurate than the particular religious denomination to which he belongs. An individual may be even more passionately deluded than is the group to which he belongs. An individual member of society may lie to gain power even more often than society as a whole. But these "private sins" of individuals don't get to the roots of the political evil. The battle against the individual's immorality can be waged relatively easily. Lying, errors, sins, and injustice, however, are political diseases of human associations which are not rooted in the fundamentals of speech, and which therefore are not necessary when judged in the light of primal grammar.

In Germany, at present [1924], we have frightening mendacity in the general situation, despite much personal integrity. The institutions in which we are immersed make us lie whenever we open our mouths. Speech is not anyone's personal property, the way thoughts are. (Young people have sensed some of this objective dishonesty.) For this reason, people cannot be unconditionally loyal to these institutions. At opportune moments, souls shake off mechanical, coincidental social groupings like these, such as most special interest groups and philosophical associations. All secondary organizations are scattered to the winds.

On the other hand, people have essential, necessary, and real bonds with the world of physical causes and effects, with the world of bodily needs, and with the intellectual life of uniform reason. The material division of labor binds people into a real world which they help build and which represents a community of coworkers. A community of people who share ideas and concepts is also cohesive. So here we have found indispensable social groups that continually renew body and mind while sustaining both.

Nevertheless, by themselves these two genuine communities are insufficient. Work transforms the world by pursuing its laws of cause and effect. The mind transforms thoughts, which it ponders in the light of a uniform point of view. But neither mind nor matter alone can transform a person. They have to be subordinated to a community that can. Man grows. Working with matter and thinking with the mind are not up to such a task. They don't make anything grow; they just change and develop things that are already there. One's fundamental attitude and the division of labor, both, are always inherited; so as subjects or objects, we are always older than the experiences of our souls.

Characteristics of peoples, family traits, and talents always surface again. (In that sense the "folk" instincts are right: matter remains matter.) Man, when considered worldly or reasonable, has no history. Both souls and peoples can grow, obey new commands, and become historical only when acting in the second grammatical person. For transforming is part of growing. Neither logic nor mathematics can transform any part of man. But if his fundamental attitudes or convictions change, the logical break is irreparable. Numbers make it crystal clear when profits or quality change. The more rationally and efficiently economic associations are managed, the faster they break up when a recession hits. And party ideologies can't outlast the illogic that major catastrophes produce. Party programs, special interest groups, etc., of the previous era simply disintegrate in the face of the realities of November 9, 1918. They're just obsolete.[5]

Communities of souls, by contrast, emerge rejuvenated from every catastrophe they live through together, which is why misfortunes alone show whether communities of souls do exist and where they do. New communities manufactured out of whole cloth after the 9th of November, be they orders, fellowships, or parties, will be blown away by the first catastrophe. This just goes to show that up to now, people have only been able to picture the ABC's of communal life in terms of the common will of a group of "I"s (people in the first person), or in terms of the communal existence of things (people in the third person).

---

5. November 9, 1918, marked, the end of the German monarchy and the establishment of a republic

10

Our People

On November 9, 1918, we were neither a commonwealth nor a people with a common will. But that day caused everyone, from Hindenburg to Liebknecht, to virtually die, to break through to a new time, to change.[1] So we indeed have a life in common despite it all. "*Gemeinde*" [in English, "community," "congregation"] is the old word for a communal life that has withstood a catastrophe. That is a more accurate term than "*volksgemeinschaft*," the community of the people, which is used to mean all sorts of things these days.

Our people is not a commonwealth and we do not have a common will. Its body and its material interests are decaying, and its will is only resentment of the foreign wills imposed on it. But it is still a people for the very reason that it is a congregation of those who dare to speak of "our people" after what has happened and despite it. But there aren't as many people who dare to do that as it may appear superficially. All those who want to pretend at the tops of their voices that the 9th of November never happened, obviously do not belong to this congregation. They want to be just

---

1. Paul von Hindenburg (1847-1934), general in World War I and president of Germany when Hitler came to power. Karl Liebknecht (1871-1919), radical socialist leader in Germany, killed in the conflict over a general strike.

minds or bodies, a race of victorious heroes or a great world power. For themselves, they want to hold on to their personal desires for victory and power, to their utopias.

A people, when a congregation, is neither an authoritarian state (first person) nor a population of 60 million (third person), but rather a people ready for its calling, and for that reason alone capable of facing the present and also of regenerating itself physically and spiritually. The soul can renew body and spirit, but not vice-versa, because when a "you" contemplates the task before it, both spiritual and physical paths open up. Convictions and one's awareness of the outer world both originate in contemplation.[2] Contemplation can renew the spiritual sense of self-consciousness, as well as the physical senses. Life in the second grammatical person is the basis for renewal of both men and peoples, and it will remain so.

These insights prove again that the grammar of the soul is not an ineffectual luxury. Just as mathematics opens up nature and allows man to control the world of space, that is, the world of "it"s, man needs grammar to open up time and allow him to control the history of peoples.

Grammar is the medium in which the politics, life styles, and changing social structures of all nations express themselves. Up to now these processes have taken place instinctively. But the talking—or babble—about peoples and souls is not what's new. That in itself would not make anyone wake up. What's new is that appraisals made in the light of grammar offer a method of therapy. First, only grammar can give accurate diagnoses. Grammar makes it possible to test existing communities to see if they are healthy and capable of changing. We will find grammatical defects in communities that are psychically ill. The language of modern factory workshops reveals symptoms of deficiency which make it possible to diagnose exactly the social pathologies of the proletariat, the engineers, etc. For example, the language of the modem factory is exclusively superficial. After all, it is a creature of expedient

---

2. German play on words: *Besinnung*-contemplation; *Gesinnung* convictions; and *Sinne*-the senses.

worldly activity. It lacks any epical character— that is, any genuine indicative of the soul which could settle down and master things. In these circumstances, people are unable to overcome strife, hate, and curses by talking about things with one another and objectifying them. Instead, the problems just keep eating away at everybody. This is only one example of the bountiful results of a grammatical inventory.

The first conclusion from laying this grammatical foundation would have to be that we should apply the language that people use at work—in fact the languages used in all realms of life—as diagnostic tools of social therapy. Logic exposes errors in reasoning. Mathematics can clear up illusions of the senses. Primal grammar has to become the agent for revealing and eliminating lacunae in the souls of individuals and existing communities, or at least the agent for mitigating their effects. A lacuna is a symptom of a disease of the life of the soul.

The disclosure of the miraculous world of the soul by a grammar based on the primal forms will create an applied study of the soul that should assume its place near the modern era's technical natural science, which itself evolved from mathematics. But the economic constellations that have arisen from this natural science acutely endanger our souls nowadays; yet these dangers may well serve to promote our new fundamental science. Research on the speech of the factory, for instance, will hopefully be published one day in another context. But developing this method of research is an enterprise of vast dimensions, and it remains to be seen whether the insight and sacrifice for the necessary institutions can be found in Germany. Meanwhile our field of study is being overrun by philosophy and psychology, on the one hand, and occultism and mathematics, on the other, all of which is crippling its independence. Grammar has not yet been recognized as a *"novum organon,"* as the *method* of comprehending the soul. People still aren't handling the liberation of souls by using the process of transforming grammatical persons. To be sure, people are loudly calling for originality, primitivism, the original conditions of being human.

Our People

Long ago, in "Primal Revelation" (*Uroffenbarung*), Goethe already articulated the keyword of the new era. In the magnificent conversation of April 29, 1818, he declared that "A few general, eternally recurring formulas, always the same under thousands of colorful trimmings, are life's mysterious dowry from higher power." Their "original meaning is always unexpectedly surfacing again." ["*Einige allgemeine Formeln, ewig wiederkehrend, ewig unter tausend bunten Verbrämungen dieselben, die geheimnisvolle Mitgabe einer höheren Macht ins Leben*" sind. Ihre "*ursprüngliche Bedeutung taucht doch immer unversehens wieder auf.*"] One could assemble a sort of alphabet of the spirit of the world from formulas like these. An alphabet of the spirit of the world, a primal alphabet, is just what we have disclosed in primal grammar. Primal grammar shows us primal things, original things, in the sense in which Holderlin is speaking, when he says: "Original to me is that which is as old as the world!" ["*Ist mir doch originell, was so alt is wie die Welt!*"] Could there possibly be more enlightened authorities? But the difficulty is that experimenting with this new field of study will require tenacious intellectual work by men of good will. Consequently, instead of using people with logical or mathematical talents, we will need to make use of Samaritan thinkers who are not being used in the sciences nowadays. In the end, only men's sacrifices determine whether or when a primal task of mankind will become historical and thus solvable.

Since grammar is the discipline of changing from one form into another, it is revealed to us as the *organon* of both the study of the soul and the study of the people. The life of our people arises from events that shape and transform it. In this way grammar renews the way history is written. How could it be otherwise? We believe that the "history of ideas," pure philosophy of the mind like Hegel's historicism and Marx's "materialist concept of history," have distorted the education of middle-class citizens and workers of the nineteenth century, and have reduced them to theoretical thinking. And so they have thrown our people into the dream of the war of 1914, into the Siegfried stance, unconsciously dreaming of being a world power, into a materialistic intoxication with numbers, and into the abyss of worldwide defeat. This way of writing history has taken away our soul.

Reaching for material things causes one to lose one's inner bearing, because the material world changes its configuration daily. Acting on the basis of ideas makes one unchanging and pig-headed, because ideas are eternal. So both of these ways of looking at history have left the German people unformed. For having inner bearing and being able to change are the two elements of a life that has taken shape. This one example of a particular field of study, history, which needs to be reborn to our people through grammar, may serve as an example here for all the branches of knowledge.

11

Spirit, Soul, and Body

THE SOUL THEN IS a total process through which different states of the body and a plethora of stages of the spirit are made to serve one particular task of fulfillment. The soul is capable of entering into relationships to serve this purpose.

From here we can take an additional step of the greatest practical value. The entirety of our speech as a people has been destroyed. Philosophical idealism and materialism have broken the naive power of speech in the most important areas. The language of both groups of our people, the educated and the proletariat, has been corrupted. Educated people are enslaved by concepts. Members of the proletariat are disconcerted by concepts and have to content themselves with slogans. Who is still *speaking* and *listening*? Given their intellectual conceit, it will be almost impossible to help the educated people. But grammar can help working people. Workers, for example, thoroughly distrust all concepts or slogans about the soul or the spirit. To them, everything is basically just material. They don't understand what people mean by spirit and soul, what these words are being used for. "Practical psychology" is obviously powerless to confront this basic attitude, which is often unarticulated. Practical psychology itself robs the soul of a realm of its own. Practical psychology believes it leaves the mind its special character, but a natural man whose soul has been stolen is even more likely to surrender his mind. And that's just what has happened to the workers. To tell the truth, we are lucky that the philosophers' outrageous malpractice of mixing up mind and soul (see the close of Chapter Two) has not been able to drag everyone into this impoverishment. The lower classes' so-called materialism is just a self-defense against the philosophers' monomania of the mind. This, however, allows us to forge ahead, offering a clear message to everyone, saying what we really mean by matter, soul, and mind—a message that avoids being conceptual and abstract and that will allow us to continue thinking fruitfully.

For men and women, everything about them that has to do with the total duration and unity of their existence belongs to the soul. Destiny, profession, marriage, children, honor, fame, disappointment, suffering, sacrifice, names—all these things are given meaning from the fact that they all belong to one united line, one life story.

One's *bodily*, material needs, on the other hand, start with daily bread and daily requirements of shelter, clothing, and urges. So from the material point of view, marriage is only an expansion of sex and reproductive urges; professions are only an expanded concern for daily bread, and so forth, just as Lassalle articulated it in his iron law of wages.[1] And yet there remains an immense difference. No matter how many daily wages are added together, they won't equal the course of a life; no matter how many sexual acts, they won't equal a marriage. So for men and women, the material things about them are summed up in their concern for units of time shorter than the stages of their own lives, or the lives themselves. This explains, on the one hand, the immense importance material things have for people without real destiny in their lives, for the proletariat and all other people who have fallen prey to daily life. On the other hand, this explains the limits of material

---

1. Ferdinand Lassalle (1825-1864), a German political and economic thinker and activist who argued that wages will always tend to fall to the lowest possible level.

concerns, which remain passing in comparison with the course of a whole life.

The powers and needs of the spirit, by contrast, go above and beyond the time limits of souls. We call only those things spiritual that are destined and appropriate for more than one soul. An established order of things (like Socialism, the State, or the Church) becomes part of the spirit when several souls have to move one after the other into particular positions within it. So we should understand all matters of the spirit as an inherited succession of souls. The spirit takes hold of more than one person—or when it does move just one person, as in the case of a genius, then it does so only in order to reach others through him. Spirit is a power of mankind, the soul a power of man or woman, the body a power of nature in man. Once we understand that the specific essence of the soul has to do with time and tenses, it follows that time spans for the spirit are longer than those of the soul, and that time spans for the body are shorter than those of the soul.

We can avoid painful misunderstandings by introducing people's timespans as an organizing principle. Without doubt, we are dealing here with a practical study of the soul, which by recognizing this order lets people keep their own words while filling them with a stream of life.

At this point we might cast a glance at the relationship of this threefold division to theology, the custodian till now of all secrets of the soul. We have neglected to do so thus far because an expert would have no trouble doing so himself, while a layperson might be misled. But such a glance can give us an important clue, by way of a detour, a clue as to why the new study of souls has to use the opposite methodology from that of modern humanities and natural sciences. A clue, further, as to why its methods of research have to be fundamentally different from those that society has allowed these traditional disciplines to apply.

The Church has rejected the so-called trichotomy, the three-way division of the *individual* man into body, spirit, and soul—a division with which it has had to deal repeatedly. We can easily now see the reason why, after our own discovery of this threefold division. An individual man neither has spirit nor is spirit, as little as he is just a body. Rather the spirit has the man, and the man, in turn has a body, many changing bodies. This last point is easier to see than the first. Materialism has almost always been a rarer error than idealism. So let's stay with idealism for a moment. Ever inspired, idealism grants a person spirit. What about that? A person remains inspired only insofar as, and as long as, he finds himself within a structure that reaches out beyond him, only as long as he lives and acts on the basis of it. Matters of the spirit are above the human level; in fact they transcend everything already organized. For although every corporation, every club, every country, and every profession has "its own" spirit to which the members are subject, still, all of these collective groups are themselves subject to the One Spirit. Most of the spirit that touches and captures an individual man is this kind of middle-level spirit, not *the* spirit, but a kind of spirit, vis-a-vis an individual. Because our souls tend not to be up to the spirit first-hand, the spirit that seizes us individuals tends to be this kind of second-, third, or fourth-hand spirit, the spirit of derivative collective personalities. The German "folk-spirit," for example, exists fourth-hand, having been filtered, concentrated, and boiled down to unrecognizability from the bourgeois pan-German orientation of the prewar decades (third-hand), the German national dream after 1815 (second-hand), and the international national consciousness of the French Revolution (primary source).

The German Communists are second-hand when compared with the Bolsheviks, etc. Even these derivations have to transcend the individual, or they cease being part of the spirit, and at that moment their spiritual power is extinguished. Researching these laws of sedimentation and layering which govern movements of the spirit will have to be a primary concern of the new applied grammar. The stronger the soul of a people, the more directly they can bear spirit. The weakness of our souls makes us dress up the oldest spiritual white elephants in the world with pathetic seriousness nowadays. As a result, Germany is currently in the spiritual backwoods. Not being up to original life, these weakened souls fall prey to the derivatives, to the "isms" instead of the "doms," to the spirits instead of the spirit, to superstition instead of faith. Offshoots of the spirit should exercise power over our souls only as long as they retain the strength of the original spirit from which they are descended, the strength to pull us beyond ourselves. Our self-consciousness partakes of the spirit only as long as it turns against our mere selves!

So the flip side of spiritual self-consciousness is stupid, empty pride. A person who can't think beyond his own advantage has been abandoned by the spirit. A family or a nation that can't do that has been abandoned by God and by the spirit. For the power of the future has slid away from it, the power that could have lifted them beyond the advantages and prejudices they have had hitherto. Precisely because it only wants itself, it proves that the spirit has finished its work on the family or nation and doesn't need it any more. The "decline" of the West and the "completion" of the West are just two words for one process, that of being released from the order of the spirit. In the life of the spirit only the spirit itself is unchangeable. Everything it grasps, changes. So all individuals or communities that want to remain unchangeable are putting themselves on the same level as the spirit. That is presumptuous. That which is inspired by the soul should remain changing. Being obedient to the appeals of the spirit we have recognized as the life of the soul. A nation that is enraptured with itself, that worships the *génie français*, the German Spirit, the Idea of Italy, has been abandoned by all good spirits for that reason. The same is correspondingly true for individuals.

That's why Church dogma has properly disavowed the threefold division: to keep people and peoples truly participating in the life of the spirit. This is exactly analogous to its battle against overestimating the body and its appearances. Asceticism isn't an end in itself, but rather only necessary to allow people to see through the fleeting character of material forms, as their time spans remain shorter than that of a soul's course through life. Limits on the overestimation of the world of the body were achieved by deadening the flesh. How can we combat the immense overestimation of personal, national, proletarian, or academic spirit? The first requirement would be to eliminate the almost universal confusion and identification of spirit and soul in writing and speaking. But beyond that, the powers of the soul must be strengthened, unfolded, and given authority over the powers of the spirit. We have far to go. But we can learn from the humanities and natural sciences how this happens. More about this in the final chapter.

12

The Grammatical Method

OVER HUNDREDS OF YEARS, the spirit has also built up its own impressive disciplines, the humanities, and has built them from the strength and energies of the people. Libraries and manuscripts, the collections of all authors and authorities, of all names and systems, of all concepts and theories of all times, all these have demanded untold sacrifices. How many generations of scribes have been and are being used up to pass on authorities of the spirit and to clarify them logically? How much of our brains do we sacrifice, both properly and improperly, to comprehend these authorities, to knowing and learning names and systems? To the extent that this has happened or is happening for the sake of the unity of mankind's life of the spirit, these sacrifices are definitely worthwhile, and they alone have actually saved the unity of this spirit. This logical service of authorities has devoured hecatombs in books and learning, comprehending and studying.

Now technology and the natural sciences are requiring yet another form of sacrifice from the people. The understanding and application of laws have grown large, thanks to material sacrifices by the people. Earth and sky have been explored by research expeditions and caravans of discoverers, by experiments and laboratories, by observatories and observation stations in labs, by astronomers' measurements and by surveys of countries, the mountains and the seas. So parts of space and pieces of matter have had to be and are still having to be sacrificed in order to master the cosmos, to master "nature." These intimations about scholastic and academic fields of study will have to suffice here. A fuller account of these, as in so many other points, will depend on the fate of this paper.

For the wonders of the people and the soul, different energies of the people will have to be offered and made available again—and they always have been. In order for grammar and its application to be worked out, contemporaries will have to donate time. People themselves are the riddle of this research; their social structures its result. The human part of a man is the span of his life, his "bios." All knowledge of the soul is biographical.

So one can achieve real results only by donating a stretch of one's actual lifetime, a fully-inspired stretch of time. *Participation* is needed! That drop of life's blood which in popular belief has to be offered up when signing with the Devil, that drop of blood represents that something which is a sacrifice of more than mind or money, that something which lies in the investment of one's life story, in genuine participation, even if only for moments. The natural sciences simulate time. They only have an astronomical-mathematical chronology, timing for the outer world. Not so for the study of peoples. Its goal is to shape historical life, life as it is happening, and so its experiments have to be rooted in the historical, political, and personal lifetimes of its people and peoples. Occultism remains a pseudo-science because it experiments with "mediums" in the non-historical cosmos. But a person is interesting only if he is not a "medium," not a means, but if he participates in a grammatically comprehensible and grammatically determinable way, and if he changes with inspired rhythm from an "it" to a "you" to an "I".

The fever that has gripped our youth in the last few years to join groups, orders, and fraternities has the healthful aspect of propelling them into experimental areas of the life of the soul. Another example would be an entrepreneur who wants to have the speech in his factory diagnosed and then healed. He won't have to sacrifice anything material in the form of money, as he would if he were using the *Institut für Kohlenchemie* (Institute for Carbon-Based Chemistry), but instead he will have to sacrifice a piece of life, a stretch of life in the form of one of the years of his own life. And he will realize that the other groups in the plant can only be made accessible grammatically by working together with them, by being dispatched into stretches of time.

A year of work-service has often been demanded, and we can take a clear stand on that from this vantage point. Far too often the motive has been romantic-idealistic, as in the case of a "duty to country," or, in an equally sterile, materialistic way, as in the case of worshipping work as a form of "divine service." Consequently, work-service is immediately seen in the immense frame work of a mass operation. These justifications devalue the process and make it a luxury or a mechanical procedure.

We can't afford to do either. The year of service can only be transformed into a necessary element of the life of a people if it is presented as a voluntary sacrifice of time, made in the service of the new field of studying the people, of practical study of the soul. The honor of an army or any other service lies in its programmatic participation in the destiny of the people. The year of service would remain just a dead social mechanism or superfluous, foggy idealism, unless it was subordinated to a goal related to the *soul*. It can prove its worth only as a means of furthering decisions made by the soul, and that means by participating. Under those circumstances, however, it would be the "*nobile officium*" [noble duty] of anyone who wanted consciously to partake in the community of the people, and that means to take a leading role. It wouldn't be a mass operation, but rather an *indispensable means* of selection. We will be able neither to hope nor to prepare for an order of the people without such a spiritual selection principle. For this is the only situation in which a person, by participating and working with others, can learn to sacrifice his egocentric thoughts and his mental images of the world, sacrificing them to the calling that he has received from his responsibility for others. Unlike thoughts, words are not duty-free (Heine). Language makes us into contemporaries and fellow-citizens. To respond and to exercise responsibility demands obedience to the redeeming word of the hour.

This new deployment of those who are prepared to sacrifice a stretch of time will probably have to be carried on outside the fields of the academic discipline of psychology; but it will also leave behind all the mystical temptations of the time. It will be fighting itself free from the eccentricities of the Occident and its humanities with their logical systems and technical jargons just as it is leaving behind the Orient with its silence about the world, its occult numeric cabala, and its magic. The new campaign, driven by consideration and obedience, will be fighting itself free and that will cause worlds and gods, senses and reason, to re-arrange themselves around this battleground of peoples and souls. The rigid fronts of "ideal" and "life," "spirit" and "nature," will break down because they will have been outflanked.

The "practical psychologist" may abstain from regarding the tormented laymen. But he may not confiscate the name and the place of this study of the soul, which is both applied and to be applied. We saw already above that he researches precisely those parts of the soul that have the least to do with the soul itself! But in fact, psychologists examine aspects of the life of the spirit and the life of the body that extend into the realm of the soul. Memory, intelligence, and reactions are the ways in which matters of the spirit extend into the soul and in which they may well subjugate the soul if such an occasion should ever arise. On the other hand, the senses pave the way into the soul for the realm of the body. These sensory impressions can also overwhelm and subjugate the soul. That is why hallucinations are also in the province of the psychologists. This is the origin of the old notion of a battle between the senses and the spirit. And contemporary psychology also let the notion of the battle rest there.

The translation of the study of the soul has gone beyond that. It can be seen that battles within the soul have to be waged against both true and false powers of the spirit which crowd in. As a result, the soul doesn't just have to choose between "sensory pleasure" and "peace of the soul," but instead has to defend itself as much against false ideals as against false sensuality. It does so to be able to embrace a healthy spirit and a healthy life of the body, and so it can easily be the case that healthy senses become allies against false idealism. For thoughts that are wrong often don't harm the soul or at least don't harm it directly, which they do the spirit. But incorrect quantities will damage it: overfeeding it with spirit, merely overemphasizing certain ideals, any logical over-sophistication, or any over-exposure to consciousness, no matter how correct. When the soul rules, however, phrases like *"mens sana in corpore sano"* [a sound mind in a sound body] can be exposed as being inadequate. This saying redraws the psycho-physical parallel of antiquity, which we have recognized as a parallel between the realm of the spirit and the realm of the body. We dismissed this ancient prison of a theory in Chapters Ten and Eleven. In these days of bodily fitness this expression is being quoted more than ever. The respect accorded it and its effect compel us to protest as Goethe does in the notes to his *Diwan*:

> If someone regards words and expressions as holy testimonials and doesn't want to see them merely traded momentarily, like bad pennies or paper money, but would rather see them exchanged at true value in the marketplace of the spirit, then one can't be cross with him if he makes us aware of the way that *traditional expressions—which no one objects to anymore—exert all the same a damaging influence, darken our views, distort our comprehension, and give whole fields of learning the wrong direction.*
>
> *Wenn jemand Wort und Ausdruck als heilige Zeugnisse betrachtet und sie nicht etwa, wie Scheinpfennige oder Papiergeld nur zu schnellem, augenblicklichem Verkehr bringen, sondern im geistigen Handel und Wandel als wahres Äquivalent ausgetauscht wissen will, so kann man ihm nicht verübeln, dass er aufmerksam macht, wie* herkömmliche Ausdrücke, *woran niemand mehr Arges hat, doch einen* schädlichen Einfluss verüben, Ansichten verdüstern, den Begriff enstellen und ganzen Fächern eine falsche Richtung geben.

The spirit doesn't reside *in* a body. Instead, "the soul" fights its way through the demands of the body and those of the spirit, never overcoming both in a parallel way, but always differently in response to each resistance offered by either of them. The study of the soul alone can reveal the meaning and limits of "intelligence," that principal concept of practical psychology. A problem as practical as selecting people with talent can only be solved if everyone recognizes that intelligence is only a means to an end, a servant of the soul on its course into the realm of the spirit, instead of seeing intelligence as an end in itself, as it is seen today.

What we just called the pathway of the soul into the realm of the spirit is what happens to the soul when, on its trek between birth and death, it reaches trustingly for the means the spirit offers it. These means are speech. Speech has also been called the body of the spirit. A soul that speaks submits to the spirit and is connected to the spirit and its domain. It is only in taking a second step that the soul restricts its trusting speaking and conversing to more and more distrustful thinking and reflection about the goods of the spirit. *Thinkers especially may have lost the courage to speak.* When that's true, they use their souls as little as gossips who have been haunted neither by the fear of thinking nor by the pale cast of thoughts. So both fear and hope, in the form of doubt and faith, have to hold sway over the vocal cords of the soul in order that speaking and thinking remain in healthy balance.

Naturally the soul has a pathway into the realm of the body as well, with the body with which it is born. And sensuality, like intelligence, is subject to the tension in the soul between fear and hope. Woe to the soul if this isn't so. For then the sure feeling for the laws of one's own body, the self-confidence that a healthy woman has for instance, that sure feeling will become a mere bundle of feelings. That bundle of feelings will no longer be held together by a beautiful unity of emotional life, but will rather cause a person with feelings to sway back and forth between desires and asceticism.

We can't pursue the path of a study of the soul any further here, nor do we want to. But we should emphasize one more thing. The study of the soul can use a treasury of means of attaining knowledge that is nowadays closed to psychology but which every naive person suspects is part of a study of the soul. We are referring to the wisdom of the poets and thinkers, of the people and the Church, which is to say, of all of the powers that have been waging the battle against the occult and the rational sciences for thousands of years. To date, the field of psychology has simply not bothered to notice them because it knew nothing of the scientific utility of the grammatical method and the demonstrability of its results—and because it hasn't been able to know of it.

Our translation itself reminds us of this. Speech is an unrelenting judge. It isn't satisfied with Germanizing foreign words or with popular re-translations; in fact it isn't even satisfied with carefully balanced and tasteful judgments. Speech demands new points of focus for the contents of the fields of learning, new disciplines, and new ways of seeing and thinking. A truly practical study of the soul, a discipline tempered in the fire of origins, will fare as have the disciplines of law, economics, and many other fields. Application will bring about transformation. It will become a new body of knowledge, a new field of study, which will try to treat the living souls of men and women found in the people instead of treating the "psyche" of academic disciplines, and thus satisfy the longing for a means of structuring society. And so this essay itself should be an example of the new method of the practical study of the soul and the grammar of the soul.

We started by examining what was apparently a translation of a foreign word, to see what popular content it might have. The result was that "*Seelenkunde*," "Study of the Soul," hasn't been translated yet, when the same old word "psychology" is standing behind it. We have undertaken a "programmatic venture," which means that we did not mind retaining the leaden word "program" initially, a word that politicians have dragged through the gutter. In the course of this work, however, the leaden typecase of newspaper German, in which the word "program" is imprisoned, began to melt more and more. The clotted political slogan dissolved in the light of the noble primal source of the word. A grammar of emerging people and the living soul grew up in place of a programmatic structure based on the ceaseless noise of day-to-day life. The words themselves aren't foreign; there are no foreign words, if one advances to the origin of things that seem strange to us. What matters is the courage to appropriate the origin of strange things, to trans-late, to ferry oneself across to them. It doesn't take courage to translate labels. That's just jingling cheap coins. The true gold of speech becomes pure only in the fire of a courageous spirit. Should the Germans want to remain a genuine people, a congregation of souls, or become one again, we will not find our renewal by cultivating self-consciousness, but rather by *forgetting ourselves*. This can let the primal source, with which God has endowed men and women and peoples, well up in us again. To participate in this surrender is the aim of this composition.

That is why this writing could not pretend to be an introduction—or to put it in scholarly terms, a prolegomena or set of principles—to the new study of people and souls toward which we are in the process of making the transition. By offering such logical-methodological pre-considerations, the logical scholarly disciplines—in short, the philosophical fields of study—certainly do bow to the tribunal of cognitive theory critics. They stop short right at the outset by formulating "principles."

We couldn't call this a "systematic foundation" either. We aren't laying down a foundation of rational and mathematical premises here, on which artful constructions of laws of world-order could subsequently arise. The natural-scientific and technical disciplines build that way, up it goes, on the basis of a firm *foundation*. It's the only way to create an order for material-empirical experiences. Building a foundation is a necessary preliminary consideration for understanding nature.

We, however, have presented neither logical principles nor a preliminary mathematical investigation. We have tried to cover a deployment of our people by providing the tools for a translation. This is a method insofar as it advocates going along with events, *methodos* [in Greek]. A people underway, a people in transition, a people that wants to change itself, will scoff at foundations. It's true that the sticklers for principle and political ideologues of all stripes are eager to torment the "psyche." They lure us with programs, goals, and guidelines. But this political apothecary just seems funny to those who have realized that metamorphosis is the secret of the life of a people. These people put translating in the place of making programs. There are no ideal goals as such, for the soul always clings to what has been accomplished and can only change over into something that has emerged from an accomplishment. Thus there is only translation. There are no guidelines or guiding principles. The grammatical translation takes effect through original changes and their application by the participants in the events: soul and people. Before the judge, speech, no program can exist unless something within the program itself is being transformed—just as no ideals as such can exist.

At the front of their sleds, the Laplanders have a long pole with a sausage dangling from its point. Their dogs run madly after the sausage, as idealists do after the ideal sausage they have hung in front of themselves. In Germany, this pig-headed behavior is called sticking by principles in the service of ideas, politics. We have come to see it differently in the course of our translation. *Crossing over to another shore; that is the risk of politics.* People have to change into new people, their sentences into new sentences. So the study of any grammatical method can't itself be a logical or mathematical theory. It has to be a courageous translation, a venture and an advance into unseen territory.

www.ingramcontent.com/pod-product-compliance
Lightning Source LLC
Chambersburg PA
CBHW070931160426
43193CB00011B/1658